Pit Ghosts
Padfeet & Poltergeists

Pit Ghosts
Padfeet & Poltergeists
by
Liz Linahan

𝕿𝖍𝖊 𝕶𝖎𝖓𝖌'𝖘 𝕰𝖓𝖌𝖑𝖆𝖓𝖉 𝕻𝖗𝖊𝖘𝖘
1994

First published in 1994 by The King's England Press,
21, Commercial Road, Goldthorpe, Rotherham, S63 9BL.

Reprinted 1998

© Liz Linahan

All rights reserved. No part of this publication may be reproduced, stored in a retrieval system, or transmitted, in any form or by any means, electronic, mechanical, photocopying, recording or otherwise, without the prior permission of The King's England Press.

ISBN 1 872438 11 3

Typeset in Palatino 11pt and printed in Great Britain by Prontaprint Barnsley

Contents

Introduction 9

Pit Ghosts 11

Barrow Colliery - Thorne Colliery - Hatfield Colliery - Silverwood Colliery - Summit Colliery - Dinnington Colliery - Kiveton Park Colliery - Newstead Colliery - Wath Main Colliery - Wharncliffe Woodmoor Colliery - The Yorkshire Mining Museum - Tales from the Lamp Room - Caphouse Colliery - Emley Moor Colliery - Rockingham Colliery - South Kirby Colliery - Darfield Colliery - Lofthouse Colliery - Parkhill Colliery - Tankersley Colliery - Mining Humour

The Padfoot Legend 33

The Padfoot in Yorkshire - The Wentworth Padfoot - The Anston Padfoot - The Mosborough Hall Padfoot - The Dinnington Padfoot - Other Phantom Animals - The Barmboro Wildcat - The Todwick Wildcat - The Phantom Horse of North of Nottinghamshire

Poltergeists 43

The Haunted Cottage - The Banner Cross Road Poltergeist - Lordens Hill Poltergeist - The Cranberry Poltergeist - A Profusion of Poltergeists - The Yorkshire Main Collier - The Throapham Poltergeist - A Worksop Poltergeist

Visions and Visitations 67

A Doncaster Air Disaster - A Message After Death - Wales Court - The Unknown Visitor - The White Ladies - An Unwelcome Visitor - Bessemer Steelworks - The Face at the Window - A Ghostly Warning - A Family Connection - Lindholme Billy - South Anston

Historic Sites and Haunted Halls 81

Mosborough Hall Hotel - Dinnington Barrow - Dinnington Hall - The Green Lady of Throapham - Aston Hall Hotel - The Todwick Highwayman - North and South Anston - Roche Abbey - The Thorpe Salvin Highwayman - Thorpe Salvin - The Green Lady of Firbeck Hall - The Schire Oaks - Tickhill - The Chesterfield Canal - Laughton and the Gallows

Last Words 103

Bibliography 104

TO MY GRANDMOTHER

FOREWORD

Many years ago a Platts Common miner had such a terrifying experience when attempting to board the cage at the start of his shift that he never returned to the pit again. The footplate or flagsheet, allowing safe access into the cage, was not in place, so he found one of his legs, albeit momentarily, dangling in the black abyss. In 1903 a fitter's labourer had a remarkable escape from "certain death" when he slipped and fell down the shaft at Barrow Colliery, Worsbrough during work on the double-decker cage which blocked any immediate attempt at rescue. A party of men descended another shaft, with the gruesome task of recovering a body, but were astounded to find the young man running towards them! Jammed between two conductor rods the lad had slid fully 900 feet to the bottom.

Four years later, at the same pit, seven men weren't so fortunate, being thrown out of the cage to the shaft bottom owing to the flagsheet being fast to the lower deck when the cage was signalled off. In his preface to *Mining Lays, Tales and Folk-lore*, published in 1916, Arthur Wilson describes his duty of writing 'in simple language, and telling over again, lest they be forgotten and hidden in the silent archives of oblivion, some of the old, old stories of the heroic deeds and noble sacrifices, the sore trials and long sufferings of the workers of the mines'.

In a sense, Liz Linahan in the first part of her book explores, real or unreal, some of the more superstitious and supernatural aspects of this tradition; and it is particularly useful for material to have been collected from modern and new oral sources at a time when almost all of South Yorkshire's mines have gone, but whilst memories and strong feelings remain.

Historically speaking, stories of strange underground experiences are understandably common in a dark and eerie world and in the context of so many tragic mining disasters. Reports of entombed bodies "turning to dust" when men accidentally broke into old workings occurred, for example, in the aftermath of the Oaks Colliery disaster of 1866. A long-retired miner recently told me how, as a boy almost eighty years ago, he had to sit for hours by a trap door, opening and closing it on demand. He recalled on occasions waking up in pitch dark, his light having gone out, "not fully alert" and "seeing" people in the distance. Twin distant lights "like diamonds" were also observed by the same man but coming from the eyes of the stable cat which had escaped into the workings. Reflection from a piece of shiny coal could be almost as bright. Whether real or imaginary all such experiences are worth recording.

There is a great deal in the remaining two-thirds of the book that will appeal to anyone interested in South Yorkshire legends and superstition, ably collected by Liz Linahan in a remarkably short timescale. She is to be congratulated on this effort, but I am sure will be the first to acknowledge that there is much still to investigate. As with S. O. Addy's *Household Tales* (1895), a collection of tradition and superstition can be a compelling record of our past, and a compelling source of information for future generations.

BRIAN ELLIOTT
Rother Valley College, Dinnington
October 1994

Introduction

William Wheater, in *Stories and Tales of Old Yorkshire*, wrote in the 1800's: 'The minds of Yorkshiremen are naturally somewhat prone to melancholy and given to wonder. The weird and mysterious have ever found in them a ready place.' After travelling throughout South Yorkshire to collect the stories, tales and legends which are included in *Pit Ghosts, Padfeet and Poltergeists*, I have no doubt as to the truth of what he said!

Without the help of the residents of South Yorkshire, this book would never have been completed. I am indebted to all those who saw fit to share their strange experiences with me, although many of these people had previously insisted that they did not believe in ghosts! It seems that disbelieving is no guarantee that you are safe from strange manifestations, as those who you read about in the following pages can testify. Alongside these tales of terror, you will find forgotten facts and folklore, both from well known and little-visited places in the South Yorkshire region.

Although some of the material collected comes from areas which skirt the border, such as North Nottinghamshire and Derbyshire, the majority of tales are based in and around our major towns and cities: Sheffield, Rotherham, Doncaster, and Barnsley. Many of the locations detailed are easily accessible by road and by foot. They are well worth a visit for keen sightseers, as well as keen ghost hunters!

If you have had a strange and unexplained experience yourself, or can recount old superstitions and legends of which you have heard, then please contact me. You could help to contribute to another edition of *Pit Ghosts, Padfeet and Poltergeists*.

Have *you* a story to tell?
Send your supernatural experiences to:
Liz Linahan,
37, Crookes Lane,
Carlton,
Barnsley,
South Yorkshire S71 3JR
Tel: 01226 722529

"The figure of the man was normal in every respect, except for the face . . ."

PIT GHOSTS

Britannia's sons, though slaves you be,
God your creator made you free;
Miners all throughout the nation
Lend your aid to speed our cause.'

- Traditional Miners' Hymn

There is no doubt that mining in times of old was one of the most hazardous occupations known to mankind. Mining disasters were frequent and tragic, and well into this century, large numbers of colliers continued to lose their lives underground. Until the formation of the Unions, greedy mine owners were notorious for risking the safety of their workers, and employed men, women and children underground while they themselves kept to safer tasks.

The mining act of 1842 went some way towards attempting to protect certain colliers from exploitation; women and children under ten years of age were no longer employed underground. Before this, it was not uncommon to find children as young as four working as 'trappers' in the airways for up to twelve hours a day.

On beginning work, the children would be given a small piece of candle to light their way. When this ran out, they would work in total darkness. It was their task to open and close the ventilation shafts, ensuring a supply of air to the tunnels. Women who had recently given birth would return to work with their babies, and would leave them in dry areas of the tunnel while they worked on as before. Time away from work was an unpaid luxury which nobody could afford, in the days when whole families would be expected to work underground together for a tiny wage.

One 17th century mine owner is recorded by Frank Machin in *The Yorkshire Miners, a History* as having said: 'Have no conversation with them for colliers hate the truth as the devil hates a saint.' Machin goes on to describe a later opinion regarding 19th century colliers as 'reckless, degraded, semi-barbarous and as living more like savages than civilised beings'. While mine owners continued to profit under their workers' sufferance, they showed a cold lack of concern for their well being.

Even as late as this century, Frank Vernon, the Mexborough miner whose memoirs are entitled *Pride and Poverty*, wrote: 'The attitude of the management was completely hostile to the workforce and the workers were treated like dogs.' He goes on to describe how colliery owners were the local 'lords' of their respective pit villages, having private pews in church in exchange for supplying the vicar with free coal. They also owned many of the grocery and hardware stores which the miners' families relied on for their existence. It seemed that there was no escape in any area of life from the influence of these wealthy and often selfish men.

Many of the early colliers themselves held fast to a number of strange beliefs. The ancient superstition of leaving scraps of food to appease temperamental mine-spirits was continued in some places until the end of the 19th century. A. R. Tomlin recorded in his *Local Folk Lore* of 1894 that: 'Up to the last few years the belief that to meet a bird that whistled at you when going to work in the morning presaged danger, had a firm hold in the district. Recently three Hemsworth miners were going to work when they met a 'whistler'. One was superstitious and turned back. Strange to say, the other two were killed by a fall of roof.'

Tomlin continues: 'Another similar uncanny sign is to meet a woman when going to work in the morning. I have heard of great number of miners in the district who would on no account proceed to work after meeting a woman. Some, indeed, carried the thing so far they would not allow their own womankind to be downstairs when they left the house.' However, it is hard to believe that even the hardiest of 19th century miners would have left for work without a good breakfast first thing in the morning, courtesy of their said 'womankind'.

Although working conditions have changed dramatically over the last fifty years, freak mechanical accidents and the collapsing of shafts are still known. Even more recently, yet another enemy of the underground has raised its head; this time in the form of mine-closures and redundancy. The once-proud tradition of Yorkshire, in which sons followed fathers underground to earn their living, has come to an end. Despite producing some of the finest deep-seam coal in the world, one of the principal industries in South Yorkshire has been decimated beyond all recognition.

Modern colliers do not think of themselves as being superstitious. Indeed, many who have spent the greatest part of their working lives underground have neither seen nor heard anything remotely supernatural. However, those who have can tell a different story. The following accounts are taken from a number of collieries in and around the South Yorkshire region, many of which have now closed. Take into consideration when you read these tales, that the men who experienced them started off as disbelievers in the supernatural - but soon changed their minds...

Barrow Colliery

In 1981, Mr Ashley Scully was employed as a fitter at Barrow Colliery, one of the oldest working pits in Barnsley. It was his job to ensure that the machinery in the pit bottom was in working order, and accordingly, he often had to visit secluded areas of the mine to repair fittings. One such part of the workings was a tunnel which had once been used to house pit ponies, a feature of mines until quite recently in some areas. Once mechanised transport set in, this part of the mine was no longer used, and was only visited by officials and maintenance men to ensure that the airways were clear.

One particular night-shift, Mr Scully had been asked to go to an isolated shaft to repair a pump which leaked and flooded the tunnel regularly. There was minimal access via one tunnel which led both in and out. The shaft was badly ventilated and humid, and had flooded to a depth of two feet. The smell of pit ponies was still evident. Such was the heat that Mr Scully stripped down to his underwear before wading through the water towards the broken pump. He began to work and was soon dripping with sweat in the heat, when suddenly, the air in the tunnel became so icy cold that 'it was as though someone had opened a freezer door'. Mr Scully felt the hair on the back of his neck stand on end, and despite the fact that he had been sweating profusely in the humidity, his body became dry in an instant. He had the feeling that he was being watched, and glanced up the tunnel in the direction he had come from, to see nothing but an undisturbed expanse of inky-black water. Mr Scully then turned to look behind him towards the darker end of the tunnel, and saw the shadowy shape of a man melting into one of the walls. The figure had no clearly distinguishable features, although Mr Scully knew that nobody else was working in that stretch of mine, and in any case, his colleagues wore fluorescent orange overalls which could be seen easily.

As soon as the shadowy figure disappeared, the heat in the tunnel returned to its former intensity. Unnerved by his experience, Mr Scully threw the replacement part for the pump into the water and hurried back to the pit bottom, pretending that it had been lost, leaving him unable to complete the repair. Despite the fact that he told no-one of this encounter, Mr Scully left the pit bottom saying that he felt ill due to the heat, and needed fresh air.

Several weeks later, Mr Scully was once more on the night shift. He had finished work and was waiting underground in the onsetter's cabin for his colleague to return. The cabin itself was raised off the ground to give a full view of the coal tubs outside. As he sat reading a newspaper, the same feeling of intense cold came over him, despite the heater being on. Instinctively, Mr Scully looked up and saw, through one of the windows, the head of a man wearing a flat cap disappearing past the cabin. He ran out of the door knowing that only himself and the deputy were underground, and the deputy did not wear a flat cap! There was nobody to be seen in any direction, and upon re-entering the cabin, it had returned to its normal temperature.

When the deputy came back half an hour later, Mr Scully decided to confide in him and was astonished to hear that he too had encountered the phantom. On one particular occasion, when walking through the old stable area, the deputy had seen a man wearing a flat cap, white scarf and waistcoat sitting on a block of wood. The figure had then faded in front of his eyes. A third man who had shared this experience was the onsetter. He had been underground alone one night when a man in a flat cap had walked past his cabin. Going out to investigate, this particular miner had been horrified to see the figure walking through a mine shaft which dropped for 150 feet, as though it was solid ground.

It did not take the men long to research the identity of the phantom. Before the pit ponies had been replaced, they were looked after by a taciturn character who had kept himself to himself, and who was re-

14

membered as always having worn a flat cap and a white scarf. Although nobody could recall his name, his reputation as a solitary soul was remembered. The mine shaft he was seen to walk through by the onsetter, had been his old route out of the mine before that particular shaft was excavated. Shortly afterwards, several other miners admitted to having shared these experiences... then Barrow Colliery closed. If the 'pony man' still walks through his abandoned stables, there is no longer anybody left to witness him.

Barrow Colliery has seen its fair share of unexplained happenings, particularly where machinery is concerned. Several years ago in a tragic accident, one of the miners was killed on a hazardous coalface. His colleagues refused to work the face alone following his death. The communication system in the colliery consisted of a tannoy which was bleeped before the sender spoke his message. The particular miner who was killed often acted as a lookout for his colleagues, using three bleeps to signal the approach of a manager. After his death, the same tannoy would bleep three times when nobody was operating it. Electricians checked the wiring and eventually replaced it, but the bleeping continued. Nowhere else in the mine did this happen, despite the communication system being in operation throughout the various faces.

Whenever men were ready to go underground, the staff in the mine would be signalled at the bottom of the lift shaft. Three rings of the bell meant that men were about to descend, and a display panel would light up to confirm this. One evening, while waiting for the night shift to arrive, Mr Scully was reading a newspaper when the bell rang three times and the display panel lit up. He checked the time and was surprised to find that it was only 8.30 p.m; somebody seemed to be coming down early, as the night shift was not due until much later. Mr Scully picked up the 'phone, which was a direct link to the pit top, to ask who was about to arrive. There was no answer. He rang three bells to signal that he would open the gates, but there was still no answer. Mr Scully then rang the winding-engine house to see whether an electrician had been merely testing the signals, but there was no answer from there either. Finally, he rang the control room to ask what was happening, and was informed with surprise that there was nobody waiting to go underground, and neither had the electricians been testing the controls. On enquiring among his colleagues later, Mr Scully found that several others had also had the same experience.

Thorne Colliery

Thorne Colliery was closed in the 1950's, but plans to reopen it were discussed at various points. In the 1970's, underground workers were drafted in to dig for a seam of coal which ran at a deeper level than the former seam. A team of contractors decided to work 24 hours a day, on two 12-hour shifts, to open the new level as soon as possible. While this operation was taking place, Aidan Caddick was the winding-engine man for the crew. One particular shift, in the small hours of the morning, Mr Caddick was in the winding house when he received an unexpected call from the drillers' foreman announcing that all staff would be vacating the mine. Puzzled, Mr Caddick asked why. The foreman refused to answer, saying only that he would explain when they had all reached the surface.

When the mine had been emptied, the foreman told Mr Caddick that they had seen a ghost. Knowing that the drillers were down-to-earth and practical men, he was rather astounded, but every one of them had witnessed the same events which led them to end the shift almost as soon as it had begun. Mr Caddick recounted the tale which the foreman told him. When the drillers reached their appointed site, they had decided to turn off their lights and have a short rest before commencing. No sooner had this happened, than the foreman saw a light coming towards them from further down the tunnel. The drillers, aware that it was likely to be someone checking on their progress, began to busy themselves. The light got to within 20 yards of the group before stopping. It then began to weave from side to side as though the miner holding it was drunk. Concerned, the foreman walked towards it. The light began to back away from him. As it did so, he felt the hair on the back of his neck rise, and decided not to continue alone. The foreman walked back to the drilling rig to enlist the support of the other miners. The party headed towards the light together, only to see it disappear into an old tunnel which had collapsed several years before, after having its supports removed. The team were aware that something strange was afoot; however, since the light had disappeared, they went back to work. The foreman bent down to pick up a cable and saw a pair of pit boots just in front of his hand. He called out a warning and looked up, to see a miner in an old fashioned pre-1920's helmet and clothes, who instantly disappeared before his eyes. Alerted by his initial call, the rest of the group had turned in time to see the figure, and they too witnessed it vanish without warning. The group were so frightened that they refused to spend another minute in the shaft. Mr Caddick witnessed the shock on the foreman's face when he came to explain why the shift was over.

Hatfield Colliery

Hatfield neighbours Thorne, and the collieries are indeed joined by certain workings. Their close proximity means that strange sightings at Hatfield could be linked to those which occurred at Thorne. Pat Bennett, who worked at Hatfield as a teenager in the 1970's, recounted the following story.

Mr Bennett was relatively new to the colliery, and was designated to work with an engine at a 'swilley', an area where two steep gradients meet. This was five or six miles from the pit bottom, with high temperatures and humidity due to its depth underground. One afternoon Mr Bennett was working alone, driving an engine which transported materials. He decided to take a short break and settled himself in a manhole with a book. It was then that he became aware of a breeze emanating from an old sealed-off gate. This puzzled Mr Bennett as the heat had previously been intense, and lack of ventilation meant that it was virtually impossible for fresh air to circulate quickly. This particular tunnel floor was covered with dust, stones and ash-type substance, and it was not long before he became aware of a sound which seemed to be getting louder, as though someone was coming towards him. Aware that he was most certainly alone in the shaft, Mr Bennett put the noises down to mice scurrying over the floor materials. However, they continued to get louder, and as they did so, the temperature steadily dropped.

Mr Bennett could see nobody outside the manhole, although the sounds now indicated that whoever or whatever he had heard, had passed him by and continued up the gradient away from him. This was accompanied by a gradual change in temperature; the air seemed warmer once again. Although he had no idea what could have caused this, Mr Bennet continued to read and the area remained quiet for several minutes.

When the noises began again, Mr Bennett put his book down and listened. This time, they were coming back down the gradient and drawing closer to the manhole where he sat. The temperature began to drop once more, getting colder as the 'footsteps' neared. At this point, Mr Bennett decided to investigate further. He moved out into the tunnel where a haulage rope went along at chin-height, and leant on it to look around. Although at first he saw nothing, when he turned, an enormous black shadow was visible a few feet away, in the shape of a tall man. Mr Bennett cannot remember being able to distinguish any clear features, and yet he knew that the man was watching him, and was aware that he had fairly long, straggly hair. In terror, he stood and stared at the shadow for several seconds, and was even able to hear it breathe. Then he broke away, jumping over the haulage rope and setting off as fast as he could up the drift. The gradient was 1 in 7 and the heat was horrific, but Mr Bennett ran for over a mile before a colleague heard his approach through one of the air doors and ran out into the tunnel to meet him.

The heat and exhaustion had caused him to vomit as he ran up the drift, and indeed he was in such a terrible state when his colleague found him, that this particular man took one look at his face, went above ground there and then and handed in his notice never to return to Hatfield. Mr Bennett himself stayed at the colliery, although he refused to go anywhere near the shaft where he had experienced the black shadow, and was put on above-ground work for a while.

Further unusual sightings in this area of the mine continued. A fitter who saw the spectre left the manhole in terror, seconds before its roof caved in. He would almost certainly have died if he had remained within. An electrician saw a man unloading materials from a wagon, and yet when he approached, the figure vanished. Although many of his colleagues teased Mr Bennett about the ghost, some of them later discovered that forty or so years previously, a miner had been mangled to death after falling into machinery in this same tunnel. Those who had remembered him described him as tall and with long, straggly hair... which matches the description of the figure which Mr Bennett saw.

One visitor to Hatfield, who knew nothing of its haunted history, is proof that 'hysteria' cannot be a logical explanation. Several years ago, a coal-cutting machine broke down and an outside mechanic was enlisted to complete the repair. The man was a stranger to the colliery, and asked the deputy for directions to the pit bottom. He was told to follow the road in a certain direction until he reached his destination. The mechanic had reached a halfway point, when he had the uncomfortable sensation that he was being watched, despite being the only man in that area of the pit. He turned to see a pair of white pit-boots heading towards him, and ran as fast as he could to put distance between him and his shadowy follower!

Silverwood Colliery

In the early 1980's, a young miner working at Silverwood colliery had an inexplicable encounter with the paranormal. His story consequently became very well-known, and aroused the interest of several researchers into the paranormal, as well as being reported in a number of daily papers, including the *Morning Telegraph* and the *Sun*.

The miner was working underground with two colleagues, who were 300 yards ahead of him. Without warning, a light appeared in the tunnel between himself and the others. As it seemed to be the head-lamp of another miner, the collier waited for his approach. He noticed that the figure wore an old-style square pit helmet and a grubby waistcoat and shirt. As the stranger got closer, his head bowed and the head-lamp lit up the young miner's face. He stared in terror at what he saw. The figure of the man was normal in every respect, except for his face. The lamplight revealed a clearly defined neck and the shape of a face, but where the features should have been, such as eyes, nose and mouth, there was nothing... only a blank space. The terrified miner dropped his equipment and ran screaming towards his colleagues. He was taken above ground suffering from shock. He swore that if he could was not given a job on the pit surface, then he would gladly resign as he could never go underground again, such was the terror struck into him. Consequently, the young man took a considerable drop in wages to remain safely on the pit surface.

Summit Colliery

In the 1960's, collier Bryan Parker was completing his training three years after having joined the Summit Colliery. He was often required to work underground at night, when few men were on the same shift. This had never concerned Mr Parker; he had joined the Summit workforce at the age of sixteen, and had never seen or heard anything unusual himself, being extremely sceptical about supernatural matters. One particular night, the shift was running as normal when he was sent to fetch some timber. Mr Parker went along the roadway alone, and although five other men were on the same shift, they were out of sight as he travelled half way down the gate on his errand. At a certain point in the tunnel, Mr Parker heard the voice of a man, so clearly as though he were speaking over his shoulder, say 'Bryan!' He turned instinctively at the sound of his name but there was nobody there. Neither was anybody in sight in either direction of the tunnel. In fear, he refused to go any further and headed back towards the location of the other miners without the timber he had been instructed to fetch. On confiding his story, Mr Parker became the laughing-stock of his colleagues. It was only when he arrived home after the end of the shift, that his mother told him his grandfather had died in the night... at the same time the mystery voice had called out to him in the tunnel underground.

Dinnington Colliery

During pit holidays, one of the deputies would go down into the workings on his own to check the coal faces and make sure that they were all in order. Several years ago, one such man had gone to look at a particular district and sat down to have his lunch break before continuing work. A light appeared in the distance, getting brighter as it came towards him, until a man appeared clearly with his headlamp on. The deputy did not recognise his face but said 'Hello' to the stranger, who replied a greeting, then passed him and carried on his way further down the tunnel, towards a disused district. The light from his headlamp finally disappeared into the distance. At the end of the shift, the deputy came out and asked his colleague on the surface who else was working on that particular district, so that he would recognise the man in future. But there had been nobody else down the mine at all on that shift.

Doug Evason, overman at Dinnington Colliery until 1985, heard the phantom miner mentioned on many occasions, but never witnessed anything unusual himself. The fact remains that many people have died underground at Dinnington in accidents of one kind or another. Because the shaft was sunk in the early 20th century, safety standards were not as stringent as they are today, and accidents were commonplace. Who is to say that one of these poor miners does not still walk through the tunnels?

Another restless spirit said to walk at Dinnington Colliery was a man who appeared above ground, rather than below. At night, there was a huge light set up to illuminate the colliery buildings for the men who came above ground in the dark. On several occasions, the large shadow of a man was seen looming against one of the building walls, as though there was someone standing in front of the lamp itself... and yet there was never anybody there.

Eric Brotherton, an ex-collier born in Dinnington in 1919, has a history of spectral visitations occurring around the deaths of his family or friends. In the old days of Dinnington Colliery, Mr Brotherton was a member of the rope-splicing team.

Out of the ten men in the team, he is today the only one left alive. Two years ago, his closest friend and co-worker, Joe Phelps, appeared to him one night as he lay awake in bed, unable to sleep. Mr Phelps 'walked into the bedroom' where he was immediately recognised, but in surprise Mr Brotherton could not understand why his friend had arrived at such a strange time. Mr Phelps seemed to want to rouse him from his bed, and shouted "Come on, hurry up; we're going to be late!" before walking out through the door. Two days later, Mr Brotherton, who had found no connection as to why an image of his friend should have spoken to him in the small hours, found out that Joe Phelps had died on the very night that he appeared by his bed.

Sightings of the recently dead are quite common among family members and friends of the deceased. What makes this story interesting is that it was perhaps with a wry sense of humour that Joe Phelps called Eric Brotherton with words he hadn't used for over thirty years. When they worked together as young men on the rope-splicing team, Joe quite often roused Eric with a shout of: 'Come on, hurry up - we're going to be late!'

Kiveton Park Colliery

In the 1980's a pump-fitter was called in to repair a breakage during one afternoon shift. There were few men underground as it was the weekend, so the miner travelled to the broken pump, about three miles from the bottom of a shaft, alone. He had been gone for some time when he astounded colleagues by appearing dazed and out of breath at the bottom of the shaft once more, having run the three mile distance from where his repair was taking place. The miner was in deep shock, and could not utter a word for more than twenty minutes. Despite the pleas of his colleagues, he could not speak about what he had seen, but something had terrified him so badly that he refused ever after to return to the district in which he had been working.

In a subsequent conversation with the older colliers who had been at Kiveton for many years, miner George Smith discovered that this area had once been the site of a fatal disaster. Although this could be a possible explanation for the supernatural sighting, Mr Smith's colleague still refuses to talk about the incident. To this day, nobody else has any idea exactly what he saw.

Newstead Colliery

In the mid-1970's, Newstead was a busy colliery with two main faces. On one particular night-shift, senior miner Mr Theaker was working alongside a deputy and four other men. They were preparing a particular face of coal to be closed down. The team were busy loading materials when they were attracted by the appearance of a light, which seemed to be about halfway down the 800-yard long gate. The deputy in particular was unnerved, as one collier had been killed eighteen months previously on that particular face. For a good while the men watched the approach of the light, eventually realising with surprise that it was not getting any closer. It appeared to be the head-lamp of a miner walking towards them, and yet it remained the same distance away!

Many of the men began to refuse to work in the area where the light had been seen; how many times this experience was repeated is not clear, but soon the pit manager had a case of hysteria on his hands. Eventually he called several of the miners into his office and suggested an exorcism to rid the gate of its mysterious presence! Mr Theaker tried to find a logical explanation for the mystery light, being down-to-earth and slightly sceptical, but even he admitted to feeling as though he was being watched in certain tunnels when he was alone.

On both the North and South faces of Newstead there were reports of lights appearing halfway down the gates and then disappearing again. Miners often 'phoned the top of the gate to ask who was on their way down, and were told that nobody should be there at all! Perhaps it is not surprising that a certain number of the colliers became so afraid that they refused to work here alone.

Wath Main Colliery

In the 1970's, miners at Wath Main Colliery were plagued by a phantom miner who struck such terror into them that they would only work underground in groups. Several newspaper reporters investigated the story, which subsequently appeared in papers such as the *Star*, the *Telegraph*, and the *South Yorkshire Times*.

Events began when a small group of miners were moving supplies, and seeing a pit-light approach, stopped work for safety reasons. They waited for the man to show himself but his light disappeared. Alarmed, several of them walked down the tunnel to see where he had gone to, but there was no route past them in either direction, and there was no trace of the phantom light. On investigation, equipment at this particular point in the tunnel seemed to have been tampered with. Two more similar sightings followed, and on both occasions equipment was found to have been moved. Two years previously, a miner had collapsed and died of a heart attack in this particular part of the workings, which fuelled the colliers' fear. The ghostly encounters certainly convinced several disbelievers that a supernatural presence existed, although there were others who had still seen nothing and chose not to believe their colleagues!

Wharncliffe Woodmoor Colliery

Joe Kenyon remembers with fear the day he almost lost his life under thousands of tons of rubble. Mr Kenyon was working alone one Sunday afternoon, in a drift with a gradient of 1 in 3. For some reason that he still to this day cannot explain, he had walked half way up the drift when he stopped. It was quite silent in this area, and nothing seemed out of place, but Mr Kenyon was struck with fear, and turned and ran as fast as he could down to the end of the drift and round the corner. The roof caved in after him so badly that it took three shifts of men a fortnight to remove the rubble. If some unspoken warning had not stopped him going to the end of the drift, Joe Kenyon would not be alive today.

"Have no conversation with them,
for colliers hate the truth as a devil hates a saint"

The Yorkshire Mining Museum

Caphouse Colliery, the site of the oldest coal shaft in Europe which dates from 1791, ceased to be a working pit in 1985. It reopened in 1988 as The Yorkshire Mining Museum, which is situated just off the M1 junction 38 towards Huddersfield. Today, hordes of visitors are taken on underground tours of the old mine workings by a team of ex-colliers who act as guides. Various tunnels and shafts have been arranged to illustrate the history of the mining industry. From early to modern day, life size models and real machinery show the developments in mining which have taken place over the centuries. The colliery guides are a source of numerous informative and amusing tales from their own days underground, making the Museum a recommended visit for all those curious about the North of England's most famous industry.

Tales From The Lamp Room

The guides themselves were previously employed at various collieries throughout Yorkshire. The following stories were recounted by several of the men, who still remember many strange incidents which happened underground...

Caphouse Colliery (The Yorkshire Mining Museum)

Guide Jeff Thompson recalls being approached by a visitor after one underground tour. She asked if there had been anyone in the mine besides their party, in a particular tunnel. When Mr Thompson replied no, the woman looked most surprised and said that, as the tour was in progress, she had seen a man working on his hands and knees at the end of one of the roadways. Had she in fact seen a 'picture of the past', from the old days of the working Caphouse Colliery?

The deputies' office, close to the bottom of the lift shaft, is an old brick building with a small window. One night, several of the men were sitting around the table messing with an Ouija Board (NOT to be recommended, as a later story will illustrate). One of the men shouted out, half in jest, 'Give us a sign!' whereupon all the lights went out. As can be imagined, at a depth of 450 feet underground, the darkness is absolute. Consequently, the Ouija Board was not used again.

Despite Caphouse Colliery becoming a Mining Museum, there was still occasionally the call for certain guides to work nights, if an underground job needed completing quickly. On one such occasion, two of the guides were working in a familiar area when they both became aware of a strange chill developing around them. They agreed that it was not a simple matter of 'imagination'; although neither of them saw anything, both began to feel decidedly uncomfortable. Further visits to this area of the mine have proved that its atmosphere returned to 'normal' soon afterwards, and the experience has never been repeated. Neither of the men consider themselves to be superstitious, but both were in agreement about their feelings on this particular night.

Emley Moor Colliery

Emley Moor was first sunk in 1891, and was a working colliery until 1986. One of the shafts had been excavated underneath an old cemetery. Several of the miners reported seeing a phantom light moving from side to side in this area, although it was empty of staff at the time. Nobody would venture into this shaft on their own, and on one particular occasion, one miner was so terrified that he ran out of the pit after catching sight of something indescribably horrible. This area was one of the original roadways dating from the late 19th century, and colliers recount how 'drippings' from the cemetery above them would come through the roof. An atmosphere of supernatural coldness was detected on several occasions.

Rockingham Colliery

Guide Raymond Wheatley had his strangest underground experience while working at Rockingham Colliery, in Barnsley, in 1975. One Sunday night, he was changing a machine cable on a face when the haulage stopped for no reason. He returned to check the switch which controlled the power supply, and found that it had been pushed in, which was its 'off' position. He returned to his task only to find that the machine had been turned off again, moments later. At first he assumed that his colleague was fooling around, but this proved not to be the case. The switch was thrown three times in a row, despite there being no-one else in this area of the mine. On the underground tour of the Mining Museum, an identical piece of equipment is on display. Guide Jeff Thomas demonstrated how difficult this machine is to stop. The large button which activates it has to be almost hammered in to make it cut off. To this day, there is no rational explanation for why the machine should have been turned off three times in a row, on each occasion when the man operating it had moved further down the tunnel to continue work.

One of the colliers from the rescue team was working in a draughty tunnel several miles from the pit bottom, where he was driving a conveyor. When he decided to take a break, he went into a manhole which had been dug out of the wall to offer protection from the draught. Although this miner had thought that he was alone in the area, he was soon joined by a fellow whom he didn't recognise. The gentleman entered the manhole and sat chatting for a while before eventually leaving. It was only when he had gone, that the collier realised he had been wearing old-fashioned gaiters and no knee pads. At this point, he decided to 'phone the pit bottom to ask who the man was. Nobody could account for his appearance, and the miner was told that nobody else could possibly be in the same tunnel. Thoroughly unnerved by the encounter, he turned off the power supply to his machinery, walked out of the pit, and refused to go underground again.

On another occasion, Brian Gooder remembers a 'phone call to the pit bottom from a miner saying that he was now ready to leave, but had missed the transport. The crew waited for him to walk to the pit bottom; when nobody appeared, a full-scale search was organised. All men underground are carefully monitored so that, in the event of an accident, every person can be accounted for... and yet the foreman said that every miner who had entered the mine had left safely. The search went on for two hours before it was called off; nobody to this day can account for the mysterious telephone call. Mr Gooder also pointed out that nobody would have been so intent on a practical joke that they would have been prepared to make themselves two hours late in leaving work!

South Kirby Colliery

Guide Stan Moss was on night shift at South Kirby Colliery, where he worked as a unit fitter. The overman at the time asked him to stand in for some cutting work, but warned Mr Moss not to go down the tailgate as a fall of rock had completely blocked it off. A group of men made their way down the main gate instead. Shortly afterwards, Mr Moss saw a head lamp moving about in the tailgate. In surprise he approached to see whether the gate had been cleared more quickly than expected, but found that it was still blocked. Mr Moss then informed the overman that there was definitely somebody in the tailgate, although the lamp disappeared on further investigation, only to reappear again later. Mr Moss and his colleagues remained convinced that a light was moving about in the area of the roof collapse; nobody could account for this and the area remained completely blocked for some time afterwards.

In a disused district, a water pump had been fitted to remove nuisance water from the tunnel which flooded to a depth of two feet. There was only one man responsible for activating the pump, a deputy who went to the site alone twice a day to ensure proper drainage. On many occasions the deputy arrived to find that the pump, which had a large handle so stiff that it needed both hands to activate it properly, had been turned on... and yet nobody else had been in this district for many months.

Darfield Colliery

Guide Doug Hinchcliffe recounted how a collier at Darfield held a conversation with one of his colleagues in a certain tunnel one afternoon, at the beginning of his shift. On returning above ground, he was looked at in disbelief when he mentioned who he had been speaking to. The miner was told that this particular colleague had died that very morning in a freak accident, at the other end of the tunnel in which he had been chatting to him.

Lofthouse Colliery

Lofthouse was the scene of a tragic accident several years ago. A group of colliers were removing stone from near the tailgate, when a heavy slab fell on one particular man. Although he could conceivably have been saved, it took the others so long to remove the heavy weight that he was dead by the time they did so. After his death, there were many stories of men hearing cries for help emanating from this area of the mine, although nobody was ever there.

Parkhill Colliery

Many people say that ghosts are either seen or heard, but rarely ever both. Guide Dick Fisher recounted an unsolved mystery from Parkhill Colliery in Wakefield, concerning the voice of an unseen miner. From along one of the roadways where nobody was working, men one day heard a series of loud shouts, but found nothing upon investigation. Neither did anybody come forward to admit to playing a 'prank', as often would have been the case if a colleague had tried to frighten them. Some of the men were clearly sceptical as to the origin of the voice, but to others, it could conceivably have been of supernatural origin...

Rational Explanations?

Some of the above stories could have a number of 'rational explanations'. Hoaxes and jokes play a part in any workforce, and the following tales, recounted by the men of the Yorkshire Mining Museum, show that there are often perfectly normal explanations for frightening events. Some of these tales are the result of pranks being played by one miner on to another; others are circumstantial happenings which prove that 'supernatural' forces were not at work at all.

Tankersley Colliery

Tankersley in Barnsley was until a few years ago the site of an open drift mine. Guide Brian Gooder recounted how a certain miner was convinced that a phantom light could be seen in one particular tunnel. The light would appear in an area where nobody was supposed to be working, and the story soon circulated throughout the staff. Determined to investigate further, one of the miners searched the area of the phantom light's appearance... only to find that a discarded sardine can was to blame! Light from the helmet lamps would strike the tin at a certain angle, reflecting back as though there was another occupant in the shaft. Once the offending tin was removed, the mystery light was no longer seen.

Naturally, the miner who had originally reported the 'phantom' was not allowed to forget his embarrassment so quickly. This proved very unfortunate when the same man later reported that he had seen 'a man in a suit' down one of the shafts. When his colleagues were eventually persuaded to investigate, they did indeed find that a man wearing a suit had entered the drift mine. Sadly, this story was not to be one of amusement. The man concerned had attacked somebody at a local fair, and on being pursued, had tried to escape by going down an open mine shaft. He remained hidden underground until the miner in question discovered him. Although the man succeeded in escaping from police on the surface, he was eventually caught later above ground.

These final anecdotes are amusing tales which show mining humour at its best... or its worst!

Lofthouse Colliery

A particular collier working at Lofthouse was known for his hobby of game shooting. He was constantly harassed by one man for a 'sample' of his bag. Eventually, he decided to bring a duck sandwich for this colleague, who, when told, began to look forward to the tea-break with relish. The men sat down later to have their food, and the game shooter presented his colleague with a fine looking sandwich. 'I'm going to enjoy this,' he said with a look of long-awaited satisfaction on his face. He lifted the top slice of bread to view the sliced duck inside... only to find two flippers and a beak arranged with loving care on top of the butter!

South Kirby Colliery

Guide Stan Moss remembers a particularly dusty air lock which had been fitted with scaffolding during a repair. The miners involved decided to imprint 'ghostly footsteps' by dangling off of the scaffolding and making prints with an old boot. When they reached the wall, they cut the boot in half, making it appear as though a phantom had walked straight through the solid wall... then carefully jumped off of the scaffolding so that none of their own prints was left behind!

Maltby Colliery

One of the miners at Maltby was renowned as a terrible 'snap-scrounger'; he would eat anybody's sandwiches if given the chance. Tired of his endless appetite for scraps, one of the men hatched a plot to put him off of asking for titbits forever. This particular miner had found a dead mouse, which he cunningly skinned, then removed his own sandwiches from his box, and put the dead mouse in between two slices of bread. This, he offered to the colleague with the insatiable appetite... who duly took a mouthful unawares. Needless to say, the hungry miner never asked for titbits again!

Parkhill Colliery

A rather unpleasant hoax took place at Parkhill Colliery in Ossett. Although mine officials later investigated the incident, they never caught the men responsible. Somebody had stuffed a miner's overall with newspaper, put a helmet on top of it, and hung it from a beam.

Those who were unaware of the prank looked on in horror one morning at the discovery of a 'suicide' by of their colleagues. Even though the investigators found out who the overall and the newspapers belonged to, it is a mystery who exactly was responsible for hanging the dummy!

Guide Brian Gooder recounted another hoax, concerning an underground face which was being packed with explosives to remove a core of rock. The tunnel was cleared, and the detonator was set. After the explosion, a collier who was first into the shaft placed a pair of old wellingtons and a pit helmet underneath a heavy slab of rock. As the dust from the blast was still clearing, the other men went in to find a mystery 'casualty' covered in rubble...

Guide Dennis Fisher was testing underground equipment one Saturday afternoon, and was supposed to be the only man in the area. As he moved switches on the transformer, a ghostly face appeared from behind the machine giving him a shock he will never forget... it was a colleague who had fallen asleep earlier, and had been woken by the noise!

*'If the "Pony Man" still walks through his abandoned stables,
there is no longer anybody left to witness him'*

*"He looked to the left and saw a large black dog,
similar to a labrador but bigger . . ."*

THE PADFOOT LEGEND

Throughout the British Isles, stories of mythical phantom dogs have persisted for centuries. As early as the 1700's, there were recorded accounts of ghostly black hounds appearing beside travellers who used isolated lanes, woodland or moorland. The legend itself seems to be timeless, and it is not hard to imagine that lone pilgrims as early as Chaucer's day were terrified by the prospect of encountering the beast.

Throughout England, the black hounds are known by several different names: the Southern versions are 'shucks' and 'shags', the Midland version is called a 'trash' or a 'striker', and the Northern hounds are known as 'padfeet', 'boggarts', 'barguests' or 'guytrashes'. The legend even persists in the Hebrides, where the only difference is that the mystery beast is white rather than black. Here, it is known as the 'Lamper'.

It is possible that the name 'bargest', in its various spellings, has something to do with the ancient superstition of pouring an extra drink for the 'unseen visitor' in taverns of old, being literally a corruption of the words 'bar guest.' Perhaps travellers hoped to appease the ancient spirit, which was often believed to be malevolent.

Descriptions of the phantom hound can vary; some people report to having seen a huge black mastiff-type dog with eyes shining red or green. To others, the animal appears to be a large labrador walking on silent pads. Some witnesses hear ghostly howling; to others, there is only silence. In his book *The Realm of Ghosts*, Eric Maple suggests that the 'Black Dog' is an ancient breed which has not existed in England now for several centuries. He goes on to say that 'the black dog is without doubt the last relic of the Wild Hunt, a solitary survivor of the pack of demon dogs set loose to fend for themselves in the wilder parts of England.' Legends of the Wild Hunt abound; it would appear to be a story with pagan origins. In the Roman version, the moon goddess Diana rode over the skies at night trailed by a pack of large evil hounds, seeking her quarry. To catch sight of her meant certain death to mortals. In the similar Norse version, it was the god Woden who led the Hunt by the light of the moon, again considered fatal to any who saw his approach.

Another old tale which mentions a phantom pack of dogs is the story of Gabriel Ratchet's Hounds, who are said to race across the night skies chasing human souls condemned to Hell for eternity. Today, 'Gabriel's Ratchets' are considered in some parts of South Yorkshire to be barn owls, perhaps recalling their supposed status as birds of ill-omen.

The writer Hans Christian Andersen featured an unearthly black dog with glowing eyes in his fairytale *The Tinderbox*. Similarly, Sir Arthur Conan Doyle, in his famous Sherlock Holmes mystery *The Hound of The Baskervilles*, used a version of the black dog superstition to create this tale of murder on the secluded West Country moors.

The legend of the black dog could be linked to the old superstition of the werewolf, which is common throughout Europe. In the Middle Ages there was a firm belief that witches could transform themselves into the shape of any animal, and the huge hound or wolf was a form which they were said to take when hunting for human prey. Today, the superstition has been put down to a mental condition in which the subject believes that he or she has taken on the form of an animal. It has also been discovered that eating certain types of hallucinogen, which were once common in badly-stored grain and other foods in the form of mould, can produce the same effects in a subject. Since food was of notoriously poor quality in the Middle Ages, this could explain why outbreaks of lycanthropy were well documented in these times, and much less so today.

However, not all witnesses would agree to the description of the 'padfoot' being a malevolent spirit. There are those who have felt that the appearance of a large black dog on a lonely stretch of lane was a protective gesture. Villains waiting to attack a lone traveller would, after all, think twice if they saw a large hound accompanying their target. As Tom Cunniff said in his book *The Supernatural in Yorkshire*, 'The Bargest is a mythical beast of huge proportions reported to have been seen over the years throughout many areas of the North. Why it appears is not fully understood, but it is generally regarded as a protective spirit rather than as a harbinger of bad news.'

34

The Padfoot in Yorkshire

Another account of the phantom hound comes from J. S. Fletcher, who wrote in *Memories of a Spectator*, 'I have heard the people talk much of ghosts but they had a firm belief in whatever it may have been that they called the Bargest, a strange, supernatural animal something like a hound, but bigger, the peculiar characteristics of which were that it made not the slightest noise in walking and had eyes as big as saucers. I do not know if the Bargest was a good or an evil spirit but there was an old woman, living a few years ago, who told me that when she worked at a certain farm the Bargest used to accompany her home every night in the dark months, never leaving her until she was safe within her own cottage.'

Again, a further account of the protective spirit of the padfoot is recalled by Tom Cunniff, concerning a night cook at Pontefract Infirmary. The mysterious beast would appear in the winter months to accompany her on her lonely trek home. One of the Brontë sisters recorded a phantom hound accompanying her across Haworth Moor, and not so long ago, a collier from Tankersley told how he had seen a large black dog underground in an old district of the pit!

A contrasting account is taken from the pamphlet *Local Folk Lore* by A. R. Tomlin (1894) : 'In the villages there are many still living who can recall the blood-curdling stories of weird apparitions by which they were terrified in their youth. The most terrible and popular of these apparitions were the padfoots, boggards, barghaists, or guytrashes. They were to be found in South Yorkshire in shoals. Every lane corner had one or more. They all had a painful family likeness. Camden, in his glimpses of Wakefield, which he visited in 1766, gives a description which will answer for them all. He says they had a padfoot at Wakefield in those days, shaggy as a bear, big as a calf, with horns on its head, eyes like saucers, a chain on one of its hind legs, and a cry behind it as a pack of hounds. This spectre was seen by many persons including a dissenting minister.' It would seem from this story as though the description of 'padfoot' can be fitted to any manner of phantom beast, not merely the traditional hound!

The Wentworth Padfoot

In the late 1960's, Ashley Scully was a keen racing cyclist. He cycled fifty miles every day with a group of friends from Wentworth near Rotherham, and as a member of a specialist club, often took part in cycling races.

One particularly cold and foggy February night, Mr Scully had finished his training and left his friends to make the journey home. He began to cycle along the lanes at a good pace, hurrying since he did not want to be out any longer than necessary. Mr Scully had reached a dark unlit lane between Greasborough and Wentworth, when he looked to the left of his bicycle and saw a large black dog, similar to a labrador but bigger, running along beside him. Despite the cold there was no steam of the animal's breath in the air, even though his own was visible. Neither was there any sound of panting; in fact the only sound seemed to be the dog's feet, which splashed as though it was running through water. Mr Scully felt the hairs on his neck rise, and put on an enormous spurt of speed to outrun the animal. The gradient of the hill was quite steep at this point, but as a racing cyclist, Mr Scully had no problem in picking up speed. He was horrified to look down at the dog and notice that although it did not even appear to have lengthened its stride, it was still keeping up with him. For a further 200 yards the dog continued to run alongside the bicycle, until without warning, it darted through Mr Scully's front wheel and away into an adjoining field.

Despite describing the experience to other people who have travelled the same road, Mr Scully has never encountered anyone else who has seen the phantom padfoot. Even today, when he is driving along this route towards Greasborough, it causes a familiar cold shiver to run down his spine!

The Anston Padfoot

Anston Stones is visible as a belt of trees from the A57 between Sheffield and Worksop, and has an unusual history, which is described in detail in a later chapter. The following story was related by Newcastle man Alec Fox, who was spending a short holiday with a friend in North Anston, in the Summer of 1993.

The weather was fine and warm, and the friends had decided to go for a walk in the Stones. They had reached one of the many rocky outcrops about half a mile into the expanse of green belt land, when Mr Fox decided to go on ahead and climb to the top of a small crag. As he was walking in between two columns of rock, he felt curiously uneasy, as though he was being watched. Undeterred, he found a foothold and began to climb the rock face. He reached the top and was astonished to see a huge black dog, something like a Rottweiler but much larger (in fact Mr Fox noted that it was the largest dog he had ever seen), approximately ten feet away from him. The dog stood motionless and stared, growling. Mr Fox remembers feeling as though he was not witnessing an 'earthly' event, and described a sudden chill coming over him. Although not an unrational person, he climbed back down the face as quickly as he could and called out to his friend who was standing below. She had seen and heard nothing, and quickly ran round the crag and up to the area in which Mr Fox had been surprised by the black dog. There was nothing there; no trace of a dog, or a person who could have been walking such an animal. Mr Fox followed, and noted that there was nowhere in this part of land for the dog to have disappeared so quickly without trace. He remembers remaining chilled until the pair retraced their route and left the scene, whereupon the temperature appeared to return to normal.

Although the most rational explanation would be that the large black hound was not a phantom at all, and could easily have been a domestic dog enjoying a walk with or without its owner, Mr Fox remains unconvinced. He described his encounter as having had the feeling of a 'once in a lifetime experience', and has refused to return to this area of Anston Stones on his subsequent visits to South Yorkshire.

Interestingly, another feature of the phantom hound is its association with guardianship of sacred places. Perhaps on that Summer afternoon in 1993, the walkers were being warned away from a particular area. It would be interesting to find out whether any other visitors to this spot have had the same experience.

The Tinderbox *'Padfoot' guardian of the treasure.*

The Mosborough Hall Padfoot

Mosborough Hall, between Chesterfield and Sheffield, is a period house now being run as a major hotel. Jean MacMillan, receptionist at the Hall, recounted how she was recently approached by a gentleman who often stayed there, and told the following story. He and his bride had spent their honeymoon night in the Bridal Suite of the Hotel, some years previously. In the middle of the night, the man had been woken by the sound of two women talking, although the door had not opened and there had been nobody in the room earlier. Although the voices disappeared when he woke his new bride, the man was convinced that he had overheard a supernatural conversation! Shortly afterwards, he was woken again by a weight on his arm, and to his horror saw a huge black dog resting its head on him. This time he was so frozen with fear that he found he could not wake his wife, until thankfully, the apparition vanished.

The Dinnington Padfoot

The Strong family live in one of the oldest houses on Swinston Hill Road, in Dinnington. They have always kept dogs, and their front garden provides a large enough run for their current two, a Golden Retriever and a Burmese mountain dog. The dogs are often turned outside for exercise while the family are in the house, and will scratch at the front door when they are ready to be let inside. On several occasions, members of the family have heard scratching and opened the door to find neither of the dogs were there. Quite naturally, they have assumed that one of them could have been responsible. No other dog would have free access to their runway, as all the hedges and gates are secure.

However, one evening when Mrs Strong and her daughter had taken both dogs out for a long walk, her son and his friend were sitting in the living room when they heard the familiar scratching sound once more, at the front door. Knowing full well that no other dog could be present, they feared to open the door and waited in the room until the others arrived home. The scratching has been heard since on many occasions, at all times of the year, when neither of the resident dogs could have been responsible. The sounds are long and loud, as though made by a large dog. On opening the front door, the family have always been surprised to see nothing there.

Rae Strong was in the bathroom one day when she felt a rush of cold air pass the back of her legs. She turned quickly, in time to see a black shadow, identifiable as a dog, disappearing into thin air. Since this experience, the family have been convinced that the same ghostly black dog is scratching at the door. In an attempt to stop the phantom hound, they have even held open the front door and 'invited' it into the house! Following this, all was quiet for two weeks, and the Strongs assumed that they had peaceably silenced their invisible guest... until the scratching resumed once more. To this day, the phantom hound still begs to be let inside the house on Swinston Hill Road.

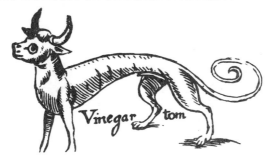

Other Phantom Animals

The padfoot legend has come into public focus once more during the last twenty years, this time in connection with the appearance of large mystery cats, as opposed to dogs. The Beast of Exmoor is arguably the most famous case. This was rapidly followed by sightings of large black cat-type creatures in South Yorkshire. Whether or not every case can be put down to the escape of circus or zoo animals is unclear. Sightings have been recorded in the Sheffield/Rotherham area as recently as 1993/4.

The Barmboro Wildcat

One of the better-known South Yorkshire legends, concerning an enormous black cat, is the Barnburgh Wildcat story. Many years ago this area was known as Barmboro. Percival Cresacre is said to have encountered a large ferocious cat in the porch of the local church, in 1456. During the ensuing fight, both man and cat were killed. It is said that a dark stain of blood can still be seen on the floor of the porch, where the fight took place. After Cresacre's death, the family incorporated a wildcat into their coat of arms.

The Todwick Wildcat

Karen Baker had been to visit a friend in Sheffield, and was returning home late at night in the summer of 1994. She had turned off the M1 at the A57 junction, and was approaching the roundabout close to Todwick, when a dark shape caught her eye. A thin mist was rolling off the island, and out of it ran a large black animal which was not a dog and too large to be a domestic cat. The creature darted from one side of the road to the other, before disappearing once again into the mist. Miss Baker has kept cats and dogs of all breeds and so feels that she cannot be confused as to the description of the animal. It appeared to be a young black panther with a very long, thick black tail which would have dragged on the ground were it not held straight out behind it.

Only when she got home a short while later, did Miss Baker remember that a year or so previously, she had read an account in a local paper about a man who was convinced that he had seen a black panther when out walking his dog in Todwick one morning. If such a creature has made its home among the secluded fields around this village, then more sightings will likely be forthcoming.

The Phantom Horse of North Nottinghamshire

There are many well-known tales of phantom animals which have been recorded throughout history. Phantom dogs in the form of those who 'visit' their old owners after their deaths are quite common. There have even been one or two phantom pet cats reported, but as far as horses go, most of these seem to have a human handler attached to them, as with the two sightings of highwaymen or the coach and horses which are described in a later chapter. This particular story was related by Brynn Ackril, who saw a most unusual apparition one misty night...

Mr Ackril was a lorry driver who often travelled late at night across the South Yorkshire border, out to Ranskill and towards Gainsborough. It was a familiar journey, and even though much of it was along winding country lanes, despite the thick mist on this particular night, he was not unsettled as he drove. One stretch of the road was flat, and was close to the Chesterfield Canal. At this point the mist was thick, so Mr Ackril was driving very carefully. Suddenly, a grey horse darted out onto the road in front of the lorry, and knowing that he could not possibly avoid it, Mr Ackril slammed the brakes on but feared for the worst. There was no way the animal could have escaped unhurt, but he was surprised that there had been no thud of impact on the front of the lorry. He opened the cab door and jumped out to check the road. The horse was nowhere to be seen. At the instant he got out of the vehicle, Mr Ackril can remember feeling a strange chill, and he knew at once that the horse had not been a living animal but an apparition.

If spectres of the human kind are thought to re-live their moments of death over and over again, could the same be true for a horse, once knocked down and killed by a lorry on this country lane?

Woodcut, 1489:
'The witches have their spirits, some hath one, some hath more... cats, weasels, dogs or toads... whom they nourish by letting them suck now and then a drop of blood'
Gifford: A dialogue concerning witches, 1593

41

"The vicar appeared even more frightened than
the family, and rapidly finished his prayers ..."

POLTERGEISTS

Poltergeist activity can begin and end suddenly, without apparent reason. Some troubled families are forced out of their homes, and all accounts show how stressful the experience of a poltergeist can be. It is one matter seeing a ghost, and yet another having to live with one! The following stories, some told by people who do not wish to be named, should convince even the most die-hard sceptics that supernatural phenomena exist.

The Haunted Cottage

In the peaceful South Yorkshire village of South Anston, there are many old stone cottages which are a legacy of the days when the village was a tiny agricultural community. Steve Tinkler and his wife bought a 300-year-old cottage next to the Norman Church, and in the mid-1970's undertook major renovation work which included replacing the roof, windows, floors and rebuilding some of the walls.

For a while the Tinklers had to live with relatives, but often returned to the unfinished cottage to check on progress and to deter burglars. They had moved most of their furniture upstairs for the builders to carry on below, and around eight o'clock one night, were both upstairs with a single light working from the only available power point in the house. Mrs Tinkler was in the bedroom, and her husband was in the bathroom. He was by the wash basin when he felt a hand come down on his shoulder in a vice-like grip. There was nobody else present in the room at the time, and since Mrs Tinkler had seen and heard nothing, she immediately tried to convince her husband that he had imagined the episode.

Later in the same week, Mr Tinkler was downstairs when he heard the sound of several heavy chains being dragged over the concrete frontage outside the house. There were no windows downstairs at this time, and the way was not lit clearly, making it difficult to see. Mr Tinkler later realised that the concreted area was completely covered in building rubble, making it impossible for anything to have been pulled over it to make such a sound, and neither was there anyone else present to hold responsible!

The Tinklers had specific ideas for the alteration of the lounge. The door was next to a large old fireplace, and to the right of this they asked the builders to knock out an alcove. The men obliged, although the task was difficult due to the walls being four feet thick. They uncovered a large hollow which curved around the back of the fireplace. It contained an old stone coffin without a lid. To begin with, several of the men tried to lift it out, but proving too heavy, they smashed it with a sledgehammer and took it away in pieces. The Tinklers had no idea as to the origin of the coffin, or why it had been placed there.

Mr Tinkler remembered reading an article in a local newspaper shortly afterwards which commemorated the 800th birthday of an ancient Chapel of Ease, built by local monks. As the cottage is next to the Saxon/Norman Church, he concluded that it could once have been part of the religious building as it then stood. If this was the case, it would make the cottage older than its suspected 300 years, but since old foundations were often used for newer buildings, this could provide a viable explanation as to the location of the coffin.

The upstairs landing of the house was so cold that the builders constantly had to go downstairs to warm themselves before continuing work. On several occasions, the Tinklers noted that it seemed as though 'a fridge door had been opened' here, and Mr Tinkler recalls a strange 'atmosphere' pervading the area. He began to be convinced that something strange was occupying the house, and remembered several occasions before the start of the renovation work when the family dog had become agitated in the living room, growling and raising his hackles as though seeing something which the rest of the family could not.

Mr Tinkler asked the builders if there was anything he could do to help speed up the renovation work taking place. The men suggested that he could chip the old rendering off one of the bedroom walls, which would leave them free to re-plaster it later. Mr Tinkler set to work on one of these walls, which were several feet thick, and removed many layers revealing old-fashioned plaster bound by copious quantities of animal hair. He was amazed to uncover drawings in a child's hand of old village scenes featuring horses and carts and farm animals. Underneath were the original stones covered in several hundred year old moss! The builders responsible must have taken chunks of stone from local walls in their quest for the correct shapes and sizes required.

When the Tinklers finally moved into their newly finished home with their two small children, they put all suspicions about the cottage behind them. But it was not long before phantom footsteps were heard pacing across the upstairs landing when the children were in bed and Mr and Mrs Tinkler were downstairs. At first they assumed that the children had got out of bed and were moving around. Further investigation proved that the children (too young at the time to be involved in practical jokes) were both sound asleep. This happened on many occasions. When Mrs Tinkler's mother came to baby-sit, she reported the same mystery footsteps. In an effort to reassure her, the Tinklers suggested that it was her imagination and that they had not experienced anything similar!

One evening the Tinklers had friends round for a dinner party. Their living room door was one of the originals, and had an old-fashioned metal latch fastening. One of the guests turned transfixed from the dinner table after having watched it open and close itself, and asked, 'Do things like this often happen here?'

The most frightening discovery came as the garden was being altered, ready for a new lawn. Mr Tinkler was digging one Sunday evening when he unearthed several old bones. At first he assumed that they belonged to an animal, until he discovered a human skull. He took the find inside to show his wife, and they decided that the police must be called in. Within 15 minutes of making the telephone call, around thirty officers arrived at the cottage in no less than a dozen vehicles of all shapes and sizes: murder squad, crime squad, pathologist and uniform. They quickly sealed off the garden. It was an autumn evening and dark when they arrived, so they placed a large flashlight over the site of the remains and put a team of uniformed officers on guard duty to watch the area 24 hours a day on a rota. Sheffield Pathologist Mr Usher arrived to examine the find, and located two femur bones of such different sizes that he assumed the victim must have been deformed. However, the police soon unearthed another skull, and it was discovered that the bodies of two people occupied the shallow grave.

The bones were taken away to be dated, and forensic tests showed that they were around 420 years old. The find created such local interest that it was not long before regional reporters and television crews were knocking on the Tinklers' door for their account of the discovery. The most popular theory at the time was that the bodies had belonged to two vagabonds or people who had offended the Church in some way. Religious institutions were so powerful in days of old, that people in this situation would not have been permitted a Christian burial. On their deaths, perhaps even by murder, local sympathisers could have tried to bury them as close as possible to consecrated ground, in the dead of night to avoid discovery. Since the Tinklers' cottage garden is next to the Church and possibly part of the old Chapel of Ease, it would have been the ideal place. When Mr Tinkler was asked by the police if he wanted the old bones returned to him as a souvenir, he refused flatly!

Over the years, the increase in strange happenings which seemed to have been accelerated by the onset of renovation work, began to die down. However, far from the presence having disappeared for ever, Mr Tinkler recently reported another uncanny experience which happened in the main bedroom. He was asleep in bed while his wife was downstairs watching television, when he was woken by a breeze circling the room. The curtains were billowing, bedcovers were being pulled off him, and small ornaments dotted about the room were tipped over in a flurry of cold air. None of the windows was open, and it seemed to Mr Tinkler as though a wind was circling around the room itself. He ran downstairs to find his wife soundly asleep in front of the television, blissfully unaware of the mysterious presence!

The Tinklers have now lived in their haunted cottage for more than twenty years. Although similar poltergeist activity has driven many people in these circumstances to leave their homes, the Tinklers have no intention of moving on.

The Banner Cross Road Poltergeist

Banner Cross Road in Sheffield was the site of several bedsit houses in the 1960's, which were popular among young newly-weds who were waiting to buy houses of their own. One such couple had been renting a flat on the road for a few months quite happily; even though the houses were old they had detected no particular 'atmosphere' when they moved in. One night they had gone to bed as normal, and had fallen asleep some time before midnight. In the middle of the night, an enormous weight 'bounced' onto the bed in between the sleeping couple, jarring them both awake so suddenly that they sprang up in bed. The young woman saw a flash of white light disappearing into the corner of the room, while the man was hit under the chin by what appeared to be an unseen hand, so hard that he bit his tongue! Needless to say, the couple did not stay much longer on Banner Cross Road before moving into a house of their own.

Lordens Hill Poltergeist

At the top of Lordens Hill in Dinnington is a road called The Crescent, which was a scene of some unexplained happenings one night in the 1940's. The following tale was related by a lady who grew up in one of these houses.

One evening close to Christmas, Sylvia Evason's parents had gone out, leaving her and one of her older brothers in bed. Her brother decided that, as they were rarely left alone, it was time for an adventure, and quickly got dressed to go and fetch his friend from a neighbouring house. Sylvia was left alone downstairs in the living room, in front of the fire. The houses on The Crescent were originally built with a back parlour, and in this particular house it was the home for a piano. Suddenly and without warning, a huge crashing chord sounded from the back room. At first, the young girl was terrified, then rationalised that it was probably her brother trying to frighten her after having pretended to leave the house. However, she quickly realised that there was no way he could have gone out of the back door and re-entered by the front door, which was locked, to get into the back room. She ran to hide behind the old fireguard which was full of drying clothes at the time. Again, another loud chord emanated from the piano, although two closed doors were between this and the living room, and she was certainly alone in the house. A few minutes later, Sylvia's older brother re-entered the house by the back door with his friend, proving that he had indeed been out all the while. Sylvia was never on her own in the house from then on, and the incident was never repeated.

The 'Cranberry' Poltergeist

The Cranberry Public House in Barnsley was the scene of a particularly famous poltergeist, which attracted the attention of newspapers and television crews in the 1970's.

The building itself was an 18th century rural house, with a stable block at the back which is now disused. The year in which it became a public house is not clear, although many private properties were transformed into pubs after the Beerhouse Act in the 1830's, popularly known as "Billy's Beer Bill".

The family who were tenants in the 1970's had a young son named Michael, who slept in the back bedroom. The initial poltergeist activity centred around this young boy, who was thirteen at the time. A walking stick which was hung over the end of his bed would move of its own free will, dancing about and rapping when nobody was seen to move it. Naturally, this attracted the curiosity of the customers, who would queue up to enter his bedroom and watch the activity for themselves! The stick would only move when Michael was in bed, although at times it would rest on a large safe which was kept in a corner of his bedroom. The thick metal had in fact been dented by its constant rapping. Regular customer Harry Bower became suspicious, and one day without warning, he entered Michael's bedroom and stripped the bed of its covers and mattress to see whether secret wires were in use! However, he found nothing.

Michael was an amateur magician and a member of The Magic Circle, the famous organisation which ensures the secrecy of traditional conjuring tricks. David Nixon was one of the top magicians in the country at the time, and visited the Cranberry himself to ascertain whether or not the walking stick was truly 'possessed'. Although this caused a certain amount of scepticism among those who had witnessed the dancing stick, customers continued to flock upstairs at Michael's bedtime to watch the antics for themselves. They would direct questions at the walking stick, with one rap for 'yes' and two for 'no'. There was only one man who the stick refused to perform for; this gentleman was a regular customer, and yet each time he entered the bedroom, the stick remained silent. In an attempt to 'fool' the force responsible, he dressed up one night in somebody else's coat and hat... but the stick still refused to move until he left the room!

Despite the sceptics, other happenings at the Cranberry would suggest that a supernatural presence was indeed responsible. Michael's father reported seeing the spectre of a young girl dressed in white in one of the upstairs rooms. Even today, regular customers at the Cranberry describe it as a place of extreme coldness even in the heat of summer. The television, which is mounted in a corner of the darts room, is often switched on when nobody has been seen to enter the room. The water taps behind the bar begin to flow without warning, and more recently, the cleaning lady was disturbed by two pans on the cooker rattling themselves! When the current barmaid opens the Cranberry each morning, she will not close the doors behind her until she has opened all the curtains and turned the music on. A plumber who visited recently located the back bedroom as a source of intense cold, declaring that it was this room, rather than the one next door (the old lounge), which played host to a 'strange presence'. He had no previous knowledge that the bedroom had indeed been a focus for poltergeist activity.

Despite this, the tenants who took over the Cranberry when Michael and his parents left lived there for eighteen years and did not report a single strange incident. Neither has the current temporary landlord seen or heard anything strange, although the upstairs living area is not occupied at present. It is said that when Michael left, he took his walking stick with him, and it was broken during the removal. Whether or not he is still visited by a strange presence after all these years is unknown. Perhaps the new tenants of the Cranberry, who will move in shortly, will be left in peace.

An 18th century cartoon illustrating Poltergeist activity.
In common with the Cranberry case, rapping noises were heard when the subject lay in bed.

A Profusion of Poltergeists

The family who shared the following story have requested that their names be changed, and that the location of the happenings be withheld.

In 1980, a family of six who shall be known as the Robinsons, moved into their new home in a large South Yorkshire village on the outskirts of Rotherham. They were local to this area, so the move had not been an upheaval, and indeed marked a turn in their fortunes, since Mrs Robinson had secured the job as warden for the local old people's sheltered accommodation. The Robinsons' house was therefore offered along with the post; it was relatively new and spacious and seemed ideal for a large family. They had not been in the house for long when strange happenings heralded the beginning of a two-year nightmare.

Their youngest daughter began to refuse to go into the bedroom, which she shared with her elder sister, alone. She was eight years old at the time, and although nothing unusual had been seen in the house, the little girl became convinced that there was 'something' in the bedroom. However, before the Robinsons had moved in, several of the old people in the centre told how a vase of flowers had been lifted from the piano and placed in the middle of the room by an unseen hand. The incident had not been repeated, and there had been no further strange happenings to report. Neither did their young daughter know about this tale.

One evening, the Robinsons were sitting in their living room watching television. Mr Robinson's chair was next to the set, and when he finished his cup of tea, he put the empty cup on top of it. Without warning the cup raised itself into the air and moved several inches away from the television before being lowered slowly to the ground, still in its upright position. The Robinsons could hardly believe what they had seen. They looked for a logical explanation, but realised that if the cup had been knocked it would have fallen straight down onto the slippers which were underneath the television. At the very least it would have landed on its side. This incident was to mark the start of strange happenings which would occur on a daily basis for the entire time the Robinsons lived in the Warden's house. Unfortunately, not every incident was to be so small.

One morning, Mr Robinson had gone to work as normal, leaving his wife in bed asleep. Mrs Robinson was woken by something tickling her underneath the chin. Thinking that her husband had not left for work and that he was trying to wake her gently, she opened her eyes. Staring into her face was the head of a 'creature with large eyes and two horns', with an 'evil grin' on its face. Mrs Robinson screamed in terror and the vision disappeared; she was sure of its evil intent but realised that nobody was likely to believe such a bizarre story. She also had the children to think about; although three of them were in their teens, their youngest daughter was already having problems sleeping in her particular bedroom. She decided to tell nobody but her husband, on his return from work. His inclination, quite naturally, was to assume she had imagined the whole episode. However, it was only shortly afterwards that their youngest daughter also saw an evil face in her bedroom. The only difference in the description is that Mrs Robinson was struck by the largeness of the eyes whereas to her daughter, it was 'all red with a piggy nose, squinty eyes and two horns'.

Sounds of footsteps were often heard at night coming up the stairs and along the long landing, off which were the bedrooms and a bathroom. It seemed as though a heavy hand wearing a ring of some description was heaving itself up by the bannister, clicking each time it came down on the wooden rail. The footsteps never entered any of the bedrooms, but the sounds were enough to ensure that the family soon slept with their lights on all night. Indeed, when this first happened, Mr Robinson was so convinced that an intruder was in the house that he ran out of the bedroom expecting to apprehend somebody. All he found on opening the bedroom door was an empty landing.

The Robinsons' eldest son, who was in his late teens, was a well-built and unfanciful young man who was already in full-time work and not given to attacks of the imagination. However, he refused to stay downstairs alone, and when returning from evenings out, always took his supper upstairs to his bedroom. It was here that he smelled pipe smoke on several occasions, despite not smoking himself, and not knowing anyone who had smoked in his bedroom.

The Robinsons' younger son was seventeen, and also reported strange scents in his own bedroom which could not be explained. These were experienced by all the other members of the family; a beautiful and seemingly expensive perfume would waft out of the bedroom and onto the landing. Mr Robinson felt that it was somehow 'old-fashioned'; although the others were not sure, they all testified to its uniqueness.

The Robinsons' youngest son was in agreement with his brother that the living room was not a place to stay in alone; he too would take his supper upstairs to eat at night. It was in his bedroom that he had his most frightening experience. He was lying in bed when he was pinned down at the shoulder by something which he could not see, and was prevented from moving, despite being a large and strong build. Mrs Robinson's mother also felt a 'strange force' in the bedroom with her, one night when she stayed. The Robinsons were plagued by constant tapping noises which seemed to appear and then cease at will. Searching for a rational explanation, they had specialists in to check the plumbing, the wiring, the guttering and drains, and everything else they could think of. Mrs Robinson even asked council workmen to check the large sign which bore the name of the centre, in case its joints had rusted and were to blame. However, nothing was found to suggest an alternative explanation, and the tapping and creaking sounds continued.

A late 17th century German impression of a Poltergeist

Because the centre was council-owned property, the Robinsons were not liable for their interior painting. When two council workmen came to paint the stairs and landing, they refused to stay any longer than was necessary. Both men reported feeling a great discomfort in that area of the house due to the fact that they felt 'something watching them'.

That December, the family were sitting in the living room which was decked out with Christmas trimmings including a tree with lights. A 'presence' had yet again been felt in the house, which was always confirmed by the family dog, Bob, whose hackles rose. The lights on the Christmas tree began to flash on and off, and the eldest daughter addressed the presence with the words: 'If you're so clever, why don't you turn the lights on and off ten times?' This duly happened, much to their amazement. Further questions from the family followed, such as 'How about four times?' to which the lights flashed on and off four times, and then 'What's four plus four?' and so on, each question getting the appropriate response. Although the Robinsons were without doubt that something was indeed occupying their house, and by this time were accustomed to this type of happening, Mr Robinson eventually turned the tree lights off to end the display.

Personal belongings continually appeared and disappeared within the house. Jewellery, clothes, or anything which was wanted at a particular time was found suddenly to be missing. On one occasion, the eldest daughter hunted high and low for her school tie in the morning before it appeared in the middle of the kitchen table, where it had not been previously. The Robinson family began to feel that, if anything went missing, there was no point in looking for it because it would only reappear when it was 'ready' to. Things would vanish in sight of members of the household; something which was on the table one minute would be gone when they looked again, and back in its original place two minutes later.

One night Mr Robinson was making his way along the upstairs landing when a haze of smoke-like substance, bluish-grey and not unlike cigarette smoke, began to appear in front of him. He shouted out, but the haze continued to form the figure of what seemed to be a young girl. She was around the height of a seven-year-old child, and wore a long old-fashioned pleated dress with a shawl over her head. No face was visible, merely a dark space. As the apparition 'formed itself', Mr Robinson hurried back to the bedroom where he told his wife, who had heard him shout out, what he had seen. He was shaking badly at this point.

53

The Robinsons' youngest daughter saw what could have been the same apparition one night as she lay in bed. The face of a young girl appeared in front of her own and tweaked the bedcovers away from her then smiled. She pulled them over her own head again in fear, only to have them wrenched away and off of the bed. This was the only time the face of the child was ever seen, as from then on it continued to appear in its smoky form all over the house.

The happenings in the Robinson household were so bizarre that it was not long before the story had been inadvertently mentioned to a member of the local press. Sadly, the story which was featured in a local newspaper was based more on sensationalism than on the true happenings of the case. The Robinsons were upset that their story had been trivialised, and more reporters turned up on their doorstep after having seen this feature. They were to receive many letters from poltergeist victims and people who lived in haunted houses all over the country; indeed they were amazed by the level of support for their plight. One woman sent them religious charms through the post in an attempt to ward off evil.

Shortly after the widespread publicity of the case, the Robinsons were contacted by a Sheffield-based group of parapsychologists who had a professional interest in 'hauntings'. The small group were invited down to the house to conduct tests. They arrived with infra-red equipment, and conducted a 'scan' of the entire property. What they found was interesting; their equipment detected that the centre, or focus, of the unexplained happenings was their youngest daughter's bedroom. The family dog had always refused to be brought into this room. While conducting the tests, the parapsychologists allowed Mr Robinson to operate some of the equipment so that the family were assured that the results had not been fabricated. They confirmed that the house was indeed a site of poltergeist activity, and assured the Robinsons that they need not be frightened for they would not be physically hurt.

The spirit, or spirits, were mainly mischievous. They seemed particularly attracted to the Robinson's youngest daughter, which is another common feature in poltergeist cases - there is often a 'focus' for their activity. The researchers wanted to stake out the house one night with infra-red equipment in the hope of capturing some of the supernatural activity on film. However, the Robinsons refused to agree to this, due to the fact that they would have had to spend an entire night with all the lights out in the house. For a long time, they had kept them on as a rule.

Following the researchers' visit, the Robinsons named their young female ghost Polly, short for poltergeist, and began to grow accustomed to her appearances. Although they had originally been afraid of her, she now appeared several times a week and often seemed to want to 'play'. Her face was never visible and her form always translucent, 'like smoke', but she could be seen playing hide-and-seek. Polly could tell when one of the Robinsons approached, and would dart in and out of the pantry to attract their attention, hiding and reappearing. If the door was closed, she would slip through it. Mrs Robinson noted that the spectre never seemed to want to frighten them; rather, she seemed to be playing games. When the family sat watching television, Polly would often be seen putting her head through the living room wall, which was the back of the pantry, to attract their attention. By this point she would appear so often that Mr Robinson, on his return home from work, would ask his wife: 'Have you seen Polly today, then?' Mrs Robinson remembers seeing her sitting on a chair in the kitchen one day, watching her as she did the ironing.

Another person whose attention had been caught by the newspaper reports was the local vicar. He arrived at the Robinsons' home one day offering help in the form of prayer, which is often said to ease troubled poltergeist cases such as this one. The vicar was not a trained exorcist, and informed the family that he could not 'get rid of' any presences in their house, but he could form a protective ring around the house with Christian prayer. The Robinsons agreed, and went into the living room and began to pray together with the vicar. No sooner had they begun, than a loud banging was heard coming from the room above, which was their youngest daughter's bedroom. The vicar appeared even more frightened than the family, and rapidly finished his prayers and left the house. He did, however, leave Mrs Robinson with a Palm Sunday cross, which she has never been without since.

The visit of the vicar had no effect on the happenings in the house. Mrs Robinson was cleaning the windows on the landing one day with Windolene, when the bottle appeared to tip itself over. The liquid spilled onto the wall, and formed the shape of a large cross. Because the force of gravity would pull a watery liquid downwards, there seemed to be no logical explanation as to why the stain had also gone outwards to form the horizontal part of the cross. Mrs Robinson tried immediately to clean the mark off with a cloth, but it could not be removed. The Robinsons later painted this area over with another coat of emulsion to try and cover the stain, but it came through the paintwork again and proved impossible to remove.

Mr Robinson recalled an ornament which had been given to the family, which he always felt had its own particularly unpleasant associations. It had been donated by one of the old people at the centre as a raffle prize which the Robinsons had then won. It was an old, brown unvarnished basket with two figures entwining around either side of it; Mr Robinson described them as 'devils', and after it had been kept in the bathroom for a while, he insisted that it was thrown away. Although there was no direct association with the old pottery basket and any of the happenings at the house, victims of hauntings have often described inanimate objects as having their own (often unpleasant) 'personality'. Mr Robinson is not a superstitious person, and yet his conviction was strong enough to insist that his wife threw the ornament away. Unfortunately, the lapse of time between these hauntings and the present day, means that he is unable to recall the exact time at which it was removed, and therefore any correlation between this and the happenings in the house remains unsubstantiated.

Strange occurrences were not always restricted to the Robinsons' living accommodation; as has been mentioned earlier, a vase of flowers had been moved from the top of the piano in the old peoples' centre, in front of several witnesses. The strangest occurrence in the centre itself, which was again witnessed by a room full of people, happened one day when some of the usual entertainment activities were taking place. It was the middle of the afternoon, and a bowl had been placed in the centre of the table for collecting bingo money. One particular lady dropped a ten pence piece into it, and watched in amazement as it spun back out of the bowl, and upwards ten inches into the air, rotating constantly. It reached its full height and came back down still rotating, before landing on top of the other money without making a sound. The witnesses were convinced that no rational explanation could be offered for this; the lady who deposited the coin in the bowl had tipped it in gently rather than throwing it in, and could not have caused another coin to fly out in this manner.

By now, the Robinson family had lived in the house for two years, and not a day had gone by without one kind or another of strange happening disturbing their peace. They had, however, become accustomed to Polly. Mrs Robinson was to see the spectre for the last time as she sat at the dinner table one evening, although she did not realise it at the time. Out of the corner of her eye, she saw the familiar shape of the small spirit pass through the dining room. The only unusual thing about this was that Polly was dressed in black. Previously, she had always appeared in grey. Mrs Robinson commented on this to the other members of the family. Two days later, her mother died of a heart attack in the house itself. It was September; Polly was never seen again before the family left the house. The noises on the landing were no longer heard and things seemed to quieten down almost instantly.

The following July, the family decided to move to another house in the area, and Mrs Robinson gave up her job as warden at the centre. During the move, several items went mysteriously missing, including a pair of Mr Robinson's trousers which turned up, neatly folded, under the settee! Since they have moved house, the Robinsons have only ever occasionally experienced strange happenings, and these seem to be focused around things going missing and re-appearing again soon afterwards. And as they themselves have pointed out, this happens too infrequently for them to be convinced that there has to be a supernatural explanation. On a more cautionary note, the family later discovered that previous occupants of the centre had often played with Ouija Boards. These are notoriously dangerous as methods of communication with the spirit world, as uncontrollable forces are often unleashed into the vicinity in which they have been used. Perhaps this was indeed the root of all the strange and unexplained happenings which plagued the Robinsons for so long.

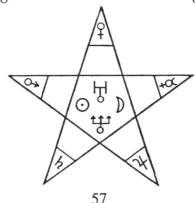

On a lighter note...

During the Robinsons' time at the centre, the elderly residents had obviously heard about the hauntings associated with the Warden's house, and several of them had seen for themselves the incidents with the vase of flowers and the coin flying out of the bowl. Late one night in the darkness, one of the old men hurried to find Mr Robinson to report another strange happening. 'I think you'd better go back to the house', he said in a fluster, 'because something strange is going on... I've just seen some angels in your back garden!' Horrified, Mr Robinson headed back to the Warden's house wondering what on earth had manifested itself this time. He arrived to find that his eldest daughter, who was celebrating her birthday, had planned a special celebration... a Pyjama Party was in full swing, and several rather tipsy young ladies were running about on the lawn wearing nothing but white negligees!

The Yorkshire Main Collier

Several years ago, a collier from Yorkshire Main moved to an old house in Bentley, Doncaster, which needed a lot of renovation work. The house backed on to a field, and had its own large garden complete with a rubbish tip at the end, which seemed to have been used by local residents for many years. When the miner and his family moved in, they decided to tidy up this stretch of land along with the garden as a priority. The first thing which needed to be cleared was the rubbish heap, which the family raked into an enormous central pile and set on fire. Shortly after this was completed, strange happenings began to occur in the house.

The family had a little boy who insisted that at night, his bedroom light would flash on and off and his bed would rattle around as though it were being shaken. Putting this down to the imagination of a child, his parents humoured him for a while by allowing him to sleep in their bed with them. However, they eventually decided that their son had gone far enough, and returned him to his old bedroom. One night shortly afterwards, the collier heard his little boy shouting and ran into the bedroom to find that the light was flashing on and off, although the switch itself was not moving. When the boy's mother came to investigate, the light stopped flashing. In an attempt to find a rational explanation, electricians were called in to check the wiring of the house, but nothing was found to be wrong.

This continued to happen several times a week without warning; the bedroom light would flash on and off, but worst still, the bed would rattle as though an unseen hand was picking it up and shaking it. Interestingly, only the father and the son experienced this; it was as though whatever was causing the disturbance disappeared whenever the boy's mother entered the room. Convinced that a strange presence was disrupting their peace, the family finally decided to have the spirit exorcised. It is rumoured that, in the ensuing research as to who or what could be causing the supernatural happenings, an interesting story came to light...

After the capture of the infamous Guy Fawkes (who was apprehended in his attempt to blow up the Houses of Parliament), his associates scattered all over the country. The King had given orders for the immediate trial and execution of those involved, wherever and whenever they were caught. One man made it as far as Scotland, and another poor unfortunate arrived in Doncaster. As the King had instructed, a Gallows was immediately set up, and the man was tried and executed. His body was left in a gibbet where he fell as an example to all those who passed by. Over the years which followed, the gibbet fell and rotted, and local people began to use the pile of rubble as a midden, tipping household waste and broken furniture. In the 1980's, with the ancient tale long forgotten, a modern collier had raked together a pile of rubbish on this very site and burned it, unaware of its associations. It would seem that this stirred up the poltergeist activity in the house, which did not cease until after the exorcism.

The Throapham Poltergeist

Throapham contains a number of old houses which sit back from the main Oldcoates Road leading into Dinnington, which were originally farm cottages and outbuildings.

One of these cottages has hosted a number of strange happenings. After its renovation, the couple who moved in began to feel that one small upstairs room had a strange feeling all of its own. This particular room was always freezing cold no matter how warm the weather was. It was situated at the top of the stairs, looking down into the hall below, and for some reason the door could never be closed. It gradually became noticeable that anybody sitting in a certain place in the living room caught an icy draught which seemed to come from here, down the stairs, and into the front room. The chill was noticed by many guests who visited the house. No cause could ever be found for the mystery draughts; the windows could be closed and the weather outside warm, and yet still the cold persisted.

The new tenants had only been living in the cottage a short while, when further events took place which made them feel that a mystery presence was sharing their home.

One evening when the couple were in the living room, they heard what they thought was a glass breaking in the hall. The little 'cold' room at the top of the stairs looked directly down into the hallway below. When they opened the living room door, they found that a light bulb had become dislodged from the ceiling of the small room and had fallen down the stairs and smashed at the bottom. At first, the tenants put this down to an accident, although they could not understand how the light bulb had ended up downstairs rather than simply on the floor of the bedroom. However, this proceeded to happen with every new light bulb which was fitted in the room. No sooner was one installed than it ended up smashed at the bottom of the stairs, as though it had been hurled away by an unseen hand.

A phantom piano was often heard playing in one of the rooms in the house, but whenever anybody tried to pinpoint the sound to an exact room, it stopped. The tenants originally assumed that their neighbours must have a piano. Upon investigation they realised that their detached house was too far from any neighbours to put the music down to them, even if they did have a piano!

Power-cuts at the house were so frequent as to happen at least once a week. The tenants knew that this was most unusual as the whole of the road was not affected: it seemed to be just them. The electicity board came to check the wiring but found nothing wrong.

The couple had been living there for several months before the young woman of the house had her most frightening experience. She was in the kitchen one evening during another power cut, when she glanced over her shoulder. Behind her, leaning against the door with his arms folded, there was a tall young man who seemed to have appeared from nowhere. He was dark haired, and wore an old-fashioned white baggy shirt, trousers and large heavy work boots. She remembers being surprised by his extreme height. The apparition disappeared and was never seen again. Shortly afterwards, the couple moved out, and have never discovered whether the new occupants have experienced anything strange...

60

The woman in question seems to be particularly sensitive to experiences of this kind; several years previously, when still living with her parents, she had seen another apparition. In the middle of the night she awoke to see the figure of a man stepping out of her wardrobe and walking towards her bed. He was tall and fairly young, with short dark hair and a small beard, and was wearing a checked shirt. Although his body became clear as he walked towards her, his face seemed to flicker 'like a poor television screen' and was made up of what seemed to be squares of colour. The young woman screamed and buried her face under the bedcovers in terror, as the apparition seemed to be staring down at her. Instantly, lights came on in the house and her parents rushed in to find out what was happening. As they entered, the spectre must have disappeared; nobody else saw him.

A Worksop Poltergeist

This small North Nottinghamshire market town sits on the South Yorkshire border, approximately fifteen miles from Sheffield and ten from Rotherham. The picturesque Chesterfield canal cuts through one end of the town centre, and several old waterfront buildings and historic inns can be seen, alongside the colourful barges which pass this way.

In 1983, Alan Chambers and his wife Theresa moved into one of the old terraced houses on Kilton Road in Worksop. The previous occupant had been a man they knew only as Paddy, who had lived there for over sixty years but had died recently in hospital. After Paddy's death, builders moved in to renovate the house, and shortly after they completed, the Chambers moved in.

For the first three months everything went well, as the new occupants decorated and began to settle in. At the bottom of the garden, there was an outdoor toilet and an old-fashioned wash-house, and next to this was an old shed. As Mr Chambers had just bought a moped but had nowhere to keep it, he decided to clear out the shed and make use of it.

The door was locked and they had not been provided with a key, so it had to be kicked open. Inside it was dark and dusty, and the only thing of note was that it was full of crates of old empty Guinness bottles which the previous occupier had stacked up.

Shortly after the shed was opened and cleared out, strange things began to happen in the house. Downstairs, there were two doors between the living room and the kitchen. Because the two family dogs would sleep on the settee at night unless they were shut out, both doors were kept closed. One of them in particular was a long-haired Alsatian and left hairs on the furniture if it spent a night in the room.

One morning Mr Chambers came downstairs to find both doors open. He thought that this was unusual, being sure that they had been closed the night before. (His wife was most particular that the dogs should not be allowed to sleep in this room at night.) What was more unusual was that neither of the dogs appeared to have been in the room at all despite the door having been open; there were no dog-hairs on the furniture. The same thing happened several times in the space of a fortnight; whoever arrived downstairs in the morning would assume that the other one had forgotten to close the doors, and yet the dogs appeared to have spent all night in the kitchen. From here on it became noticeable that both dogs would only go into the room when accompanied. Eventually, Mr Chambers made the point of making sure the doors were shut before he went to bed, so that there could be no mistake. He got up a couple of times in the night and they remained shut. But, the following morning, they were open again.

One evening, the couple were in the living room when the dogs suddenly became alert and followed something across the room with their eyes. They looked towards the fireplace and then whatever they were watching seemed to vanish and they settled down again. At the time, the window had no net curtains and there was a street lamp outside the house, so it could clearly be seen that they were not looking at something outside. From then on, this continued to happen once every few days between the hours of seven and nine o'clock at night.

Mr Chambers was a member of the Worksop Territorial Army, and every week he travelled into town on a certain evening for meetings. One such night he arrived home afterwards at the usual time, but was surprised to find that the front door was locked. He knocked and waited, and eventually his wife came to the door and asked who was there before letting him in. She was rather upset, and accused her husband of 'messing about' behind the door and making noises to frighten her. Earlier on she had assumed that local children were playing a joke on her, by opening the letterbox and moaning through it. She had heard the sound of a human voice wailing continuously. Mrs

Chambers had opened the door and run down the passage which led to the back door in the hope of catching whoever it was, but nobody was there. Her husband pointed out that there was nowhere else for anyone to hide, and if it had been him or any other trickster then she would have found them straight away.

Not long afterwards, the Chambers were disturbed late one night by a loud humming noise. On investigation, they traced the sound to their bedroom and found the hoover switched on with its flex stretched as far as it could go, in the middle of the room. Neither of them had been in the bedroom since they arrived home that evening, and the hoover had certainly not been left on, or anywhere near the centre of the room.

By this time, the Chambers knew that they could not explain away such a variety of strange happenings, and decided they must live in a haunted house. But even though they were now aware that unaccountable things were happening, this did not seem to appease whatever was causing them...

Shortly afterwards, they invited some friends round for a party, and sat chatting over drinks in the living room. One of the guests went upstairs to the bathroom, and it wasn't until a quarter of an hour had elapsed that the others realised she had been gone for rather too long. They became quiet and during the lull in conversation, realised that shouting was coming from the bathroom. Mr Chambers and several of the guests rushed upstairs and opened the bathroom door to find the guest sitting on the edge of the bath sobbing hysterically. She began to accuse her husband (who had been seated downstairs with the others at the time) of 'playing tricks' on her. It wasn't until she was taken downstairs and calmed down that she was able to relate what had happened. She had been opening the bathroom door to leave when something had snatched it out of her hand and slammed it shut. At first, thinking that it was her husband messing around, the woman made a quick remark and tried to open the door once more. The same thing happened again; the door was no more than three inches open when it was violently pulled from her hand and slammed shut. She braced her arm against the wall and began to pull. This time the door remained closed and shook as though someone was rattling it from the outside.

She was unable to get out for the quarter of an hour it took for the others to realise that she was missing and free her from the outside.

The party checked the latch to the bathroom door, which had never stuck before, but they found it in good working order. The incident remained unexplained.

Decorating and alterations were still being completed by the Chambers, and shortly after this occurrence, there was another which led to their most gruesome discovery yet. As was common with early 20th century terraces, the houses on Kilton Road had attics. The attic rooms were quite large, but theirs had previously been partitioned off into two smaller rooms. The Chambers decided to knock out the partition and restore the attic to one large room. Mrs Chambers was removing the old floorboards one day when she found a Victorian coin. Hoping to find other things of interest, she continued to remove floorboards and eventually found a parcel of newspaper tied with string. The newspaper was part of the *Rotherham Star* dated 1957, and she decided to leave the find until her husband returned.

Some years previously, Mr Chambers had been employed by a local funeral service. He had dug graves and had also been responsible for cremations. When he arrived home later that night and opened the paper parcel his wife gave to him, he was in no doubt as to what he saw. Inside the packet was about half a pound in weight of human ashes.

The Chambers had no idea what to do with the find, and their immediate reaction was to replace the parcel back where it had come from, underneath the floor boards. They realised that the ashes did not belong to Paddy (the previous owner of the house) since he had died in hospital, and in the 1980's as opposed to the 1950's, when the newspaper dated from. However, they knew nothing of Paddy's life, and were not aware if he had ever been married, had children or had always lived alone. Neither did they know anything of his friends or his lifestyle, or even if he had been responsible for hiding the ashes. This left them with no leads as to the nature of their discovery.

Determined to get to the bottom of the mystery, Mr Chambers had an idea. One of his acquaintances from Worksop T.A. was particularly sensitive to ghostly presences, and was a regular at the local Spiritualist Church. Mr Chambers decided to invite him and his wife down on the pretext of a meal and a drink, without having filled either of them in on the happenings at the house. If there truly was a presence in the house on Kilton Road, then perhaps it would choose to reveal itself to a sensitive person such as his colleague.

The invitations were issued, and a date was set. Shortly after the couple arrived, the Chambers asked if they would like to be shown round the house. They finally arrived in the attic, which was still unfinished although the partition had now been removed. It was the middle of summer and it had been an extremely hot day. The old house had a traditional grey slate roof which soaked up the heat and held it in, and with no proper ventilation the attic was still very hot even though it was the middle of the evening. Mr Chambers deliberately tried to guide the guests over the very spot where the ashes had been replaced underneath the floorboards. As he passed over, the man suddenly paused and remarked on the chill of the attic. As he did so, he turned round and looked at the floor and the surrounding area of the spot where the parcel of ashes was still hidden.

His wife refused to go any further than the door, also commenting on the 'feeling' of the room, and she and Mrs Chambers left to go downstairs. Mr Chamber's friend then proceeded to ask why he had been asked to visit the attic, but was still told nothing. Eventually, after staring out of the attic window for a while, he asked if there had ever been any 'strange happenings' in the house. At this point, Mr Chambers decided to confess, and proceeded to pull up the loose floorboards revealing the parcel of ashes. The man unwrapped them and immediately took them to the window, opened it, and cast them out onto the breeze, where they scattered. He too had felt that they were human remains.

Although the residents never discovered the true story behind the house's strange happenings, or the ashes, from then on the house seemed to be more peaceful. Even so, the Chambers had already decided to sell up and move on. Their experiences had been enough to effectively drive them out of the house. They never found out whether the new residents experienced anything strange after having moved in. As Mr Chambers said, it seemed as though their attention had been drawn to discovering the ashes and 'setting them free'. Perhaps an earthbound soul had been released once and for all, and the house on Kilton Road now remains at peace.

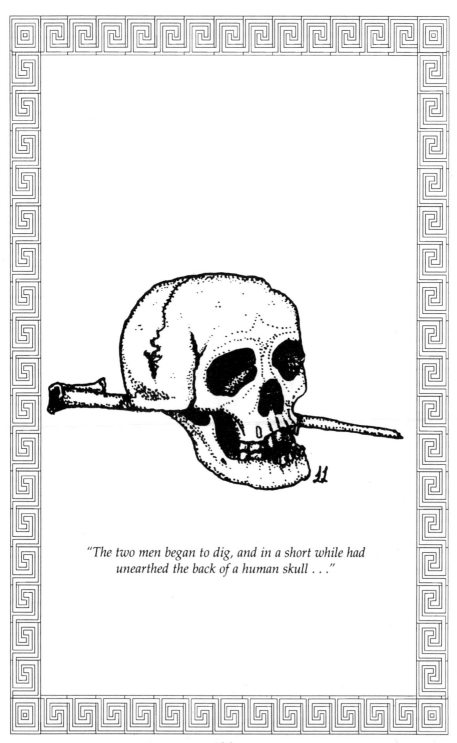

"The two men began to dig, and in a short while had unearthed the back of a human skull . . ."

VISIONS AND VISITATIONS

A variety of stories is recounted in the following section; from visitors of the spirit world, to visions of ghostly presences who carry a hidden message...

A Doncaster Air Disaster

Aidan Caddick lives in the Dunscroft area of Doncaster, which was once the site of a Medieval monastery, now situated underneath a modern housing estate. Evidence has been found to show that this area was occupied as long ago as the Neolithic period. The Romans found the site appealing enough to set up camp here thousands of years later, and coins from the time of Charles I have been found alongside Roman artefacts in and around the village. However, rather than sporting an ancient ghost, as its history would perhaps suggest, a farm close to Dunscroft holds another altogether more modern and tragic secret...

Mr Caddick was nine years old when a Halifax Mark II bomber took off from Lindholme in Doncaster, to head for Germany during the Second World War, and crashed in a field close to where he lived, killing all seven of the crew. The year was 1944, and the site of the old aerodrome now hosts Lindholme prison. According to reports by the locals, although officials came to remove the engines and the bodies of the crew, their operation was not entirely successful. The force of impact had been such that remains of the poor men were being stumbled across for many weeks afterwards, in and around the field. The cause of the crash was put down to an error in judgement either by the pilot or co-pilot during operating the undercarriage wheels. It seems likely that the controls were not worked successfully, leading to a poor runway take-off which caused the bomber to nose-dive after not attaining sufficient height. The incident lingered for many years in the minds of the local people, and indeed it was something which Mr Caddick could not forget.

Many years later, Mr Caddick was visited by a friend who had become farm manager on an estate which included the field in which the Halifax had crashed. He told Mr Caddick that he had been ploughing the forty-acre field with a powerful tractor when, without warning, the engine had stopped. Both men returned to the field and began to search the ground where the tractor's engine had seized, hoping to be enlightened as to the cause. It did not take long for them to unearth bent and broken pieces of aluminium, followed by bullets. Both men were aware that they had begun to dig up the remains of the Halifax, which must have been buried in the earth for many years. Mr Caddick was beset by an uneasy feeling, as though he was 'doing something he shouldn't be doing'. He returned home to telephone the Yorkshire airbase, RAF Finningley, to notify them of his discovery.

The Squadron Leader he spoke to informed him that no designated War Grave was recorded at the Doncaster farm, and so digging in the area was permitted and could lead to no harm.

The contact from RAF Finningley put Mr Caddick in touch with a local group of enthusiasts from the Yorkshire Aviation Society. Several men came along to view the unearthed remains in the field, and put forward a proposal to excavate the area and remove everything which was left. However, the farm manager was afraid that this would interfere with his crop rota, and so they were unable to do so.

Having reached something of a stalemate but being curious as to the presence of the remains, Mr Caddick decided to enlist the help of another friend, and visited the site again. The two men began to dig, and in a short while had unearthed the back of a human skull, followed by lower-leg and thigh bones. It was enough to convince them that despite the fact the field was not a designated War Grave, some of the bodies had never been properly laid to rest. They unearthed an oxygen cylinder in such perfect condition that the Yorkshire Aviation Society came shortly afterwards to take it away. On the day they had begun digging, both men took home some bullets and parts of the fuselage as souvenirs.

Mr Caddick went to work as normal the following day, only to return home to find his wife rather upset, saying that their daughter, who was eighteen at the time, had 'seen a ghost'. The young woman had known nothing about her father's discovery the previous day, and yet swore that she had been woken in the night by the figure of a man in World War Two flying gear, standing at the end of her bed. She described in great detail his flying jacket and old-fashioned leather hat, despite having no previous knowledge of such early RAF uniforms.

The box containing Mr Caddick's finds from the Halifax crash site was kept in the kitchen. Within a few days of its being left there, Mrs Caddick insisted that it was taken outside, because she was experiencing 'chills' whenever she walked past it. Although the family still have this box in their possession, it has now been relegated to an outhouse.

A Halifax Bomber, of the same type as the ill-fated plane which crashed into a Doncaster field.

Further attempts by Mr Caddick in more recent years to locate the spot where the Halifax came down have been unfruitful. The field is a large one, and the soil once more swallowed up its previously unearthed secrets. Mr Caddick has flown over the area twice in his ongoing quest; once with a friend who owned a motorised glider, unsuccessfully. The second time he requested a ride with a woman who was the air traffic controller at Doncaster Gliding Club. They had reached the field, when Mr Caddick explained what he was looking for, and she banked away instantly and refused to go any further, taking the plane back to the landing strip at once. The old site of the Lindholme runway which the Halifax was launched from was visible in the air, directly in line with the field into which it crashed.

Whether a full excavation of the site will be permitted within the next few years is not yet known. With firm proof that bodies of the crash victims have not been properly laid to rest, one would hope so. Perhaps this was what the RAF spectre was hoping to achieve, when he appeared to Mr Caddick's young daughter in the early 1980's.

A Message after Death

Many people have 'seen' the spirits of family members who have long since died, often when they themselves are critically ill in hospital. It is as though familiar faces reappear at crisis-points within a person's life, almost to reassure them. On several occasions this happened to Ethel Evans, as she lay in hospital wards in Rotherham. However, her most unusual and tragic tale centred around something which happened when she was in fact well, in the early 1970's. Mrs Evans' son Brian had been ill in hospital for some time, although he was young and previously fit so nobody saw any reason why he should not recover. One particular morning, Mrs Evans planned to visit her son after doing her weekly shopping, and set out quite early to be finished in good time.

As she was walking down the road, she noticed out of the corner of her eye that a dark shadow had appeared at her right-hand side. Thinking that something black had 'stuck' to her arm, she tried to brush it away, but realised that nothing was there. She continued to walk, but the impression of something black at her right hand side persisted. However, each time as she turned around to look, there was nothing there. Eventually, Mrs Evans realised that a black shadow was 'following' her, although it did not seem to be visible to any of the people she passed in the street. She began to be afraid that something had happened, and that the shadow was a warning. On her return home, Mrs Evans was informed that her son had died in hospital only twenty minutes before, the exact time at which the black shadow appeared to be following her.

Wales Court

The following tale was recounted by Aston builder Robert Lenton, who recently worked at the Wales Court complex in Kiveton.

Wales Court was once an old hospital, but after its closure, the property was sectioned off into several houses to be sold as private residential accommodation. Mr Lenton was asked to help with renovation work in one of these new units. In this particular house, the main cellar had been split into three rooms: a food store, a food preparation area, and a wine cellar. They were beautiful old stone rooms with carved oak doors of a great age. Mr Lenton's job was to chip the old rendering off the walls, ready to be replaced. Only one of the other units had already been sold, so the area was fairly deserted, and Mr Lenton's colleague was upstairs involved in other work.

As he chiselled away at a wall, Mr Lenton was suddenly aware of a change in temperature - the cellar had been plunged into icy coldness. He described how the hair on the back of his neck suddenly stood on end, and he stopped work to turn around and see whether a window had been opened. As he turned, there was such an overpowering smell of tobacco, it was as though somebody had blown pipe smoke into his face from inches away. There was nobody there, and neither could the coldness be attributed to the opening of a window.

Mr Lenton ran upstairs into the kitchen to find his colleague making a cup of tea. At first he was suspicious that the man had somehow played a trick on him, but this would have been impossible. The pair went down to the cellar to investigate together, but there was no trace of the phantom pipe smoke, and the temperature had once more returned to normal. On further investigation, Mr Lenton was told that the ghost of an old hospital gardener was rumoured to haunt the house and grounds. Needless to say, this gentleman had smoked a pipe.

The Unknown Visitor

Sheffield man Richard Murton carried the tale of an unexpected visitor back with him from his student days in Lancashire. Mr Murton was living at the time in rented accommodation, in an old house in Manchester. One night he retired to bed as normal, but had an extremely vivid dream. In the dream, a door appeared in the back of the wardrobe in his bedroom. It opened, and a man in his thirties, with dark hair and a beard and wearing a yellow tee-shirt and jeans, walked out into the bedroom. The following day, Mr Murton recalled the dream in amusement, but thought no more about it.

One night later in the following week, he went to bed once more to fall into a vivid dream. This time, he dreamed that he went into the living room in the middle of the night to watch television. He turned the set on, but there was no picture. Suddenly, the man who had appeared in his previous dream entered the room. His description was exactly as before, and he again wore a yellow tee-shirt and jeans. In the dream, the stranger looked at Mr Murton and asked: "What are you doing in here at this time of night? There's nothing on the telly, you'd better go back to bed!" Mr Murton duly went back to bed and cannot remember dreaming anything further that night. He awoke the next day, again remarking on the strangeness of the second dream, but thought no more about it... until one of the men he shared the house with asked what he had been doing in the middle of the night. Puzzled, Mr Murton enquired further, to find out that he had woken his friend in the small hours of the morning by going into the living room and turning on the television.

The friend had then heard a conversation between Mr Murton and another man, before hearing him return to his bedroom. As if this was not chilling enough, a girlfriend of one of the other lodgers was woken later that week in the small hours by a man in a yellow tee-shirt and jeans. He opened the door of the bedroom she was staying in, saw her lying in bed, and said: 'Sorry! Wrong room!' before disappearing again. The woman had no knowledge of Mr Murton's dreams, or of the conversation that had taken place between him and the other lodger regarding his previous 'sleepwalking'. Indeed, until further enquiry, she had thought that the stranger was just another tenant in the house!

The White Ladies

Clarice Chadderton lives alone in a new housing complex in the Rotherham area called Chindit Court. One night she had arrived home late after an evening out, and at around 2 a.m. when she got into bed she turned over to face her bedroom door, which was always left open and looks out towards the outer door. The figure of a young woman dressed in white was standing between the bedroom door and the outer door. Mrs Chadderton was aware that the woman had appeared in spirit rather than in person, and was struck by her fair hair and beauty, and her friendly smile. As she looked at the figure, it appeared to fade, and Mrs Chadderton, who had felt no fear, turned over and went to sleep.

When she awoke the next morning, her mental picture of the woman was as clear as it had been the night before, and she knew without a doubt that she had not been dreaming. A few weeks later, Mrs Chadderton went to bed as normal to wake again at around 2 a.m. in the morning. She saw, just outside her bedroom door, another figure of a young and beautiful woman dressed in white with fair hair, although different from the first one. This time she was only visible from the waist up. Again, Mrs Chadderton felt no fear and turned over to go to sleep, at which point she sensed that the woman had disappeared.

Shortly afterwards, Mrs Chadderton awoke for a third time in the small hours of the morning. This time she turned to face her wall and saw, at the end of her bed, a third young woman, this time with dark hair but again with a lovely smile. Although this apparition was closer to her than either of the other two had been, only her head and shoulders were visible. She appeared to be sitting at the end of the bed. For a third time, Mrs Chadderton turned over and went to sleep, remarking later that after her three 'visitations' she had slept more soundly than she had done for a long time.

Following these three similar experiences, Mrs Chadderton decided to make some enquiries at one of the local spiritualist churches as to the nature of her sightings. She was told that she had seen a vision from the spirit world, and that she should be honoured by such a visit. The medium she spoke to suggested that the three women were in some way 'preparing for her coming'. The experiences left her surprised that she had felt no fear, and the three beautiful ladies are something which Mrs Chadderton will never forget.

An Unwelcome Visitor

Pat Bennett and his family moved to a house in Dunscroft, Doncaster, following the death of its previous owner. Although Mr Bennett never had a 'bad' feeling in association with the presence which was felt there on many occasions, it eventually forced the family to move elsewhere.

The Bennetts were plagued by the continual appearance of a mysterious old gentleman. He could be heard shuffling around in rooms in which none of the family were present, and was heard whistling to himself on many occasions. The old gentleman walked past Mrs Bennett while she was ironing one day, and appeared in such clarity that she was able to give a vivid description to her neighbours, who identified him as the previous - and deceased - occupant of the house! Although not disruptive in his activity, cupboard doors were opened and closed by an apparently unseen hand, and the Bennetts' daughter was often heard talking to a companion whom nobody else could see. Concerned for their children, the Bennetts decided to sell the house and move on. Perhaps the current occupants of the house in Dunscroft have seen their resident gentleman; it would appear that he was loath to leave his home, even after death.

Bessemer Steelworks

Carlisle Street, in Sheffield, was once the base of the old Bessemer Steelworks. Several years ago Brynn Ackril was a floor worker in the building. He and his colleagues often had to take material to the Director's office, which was situated on the third floor. The cleaners refused to go in to this particular room because the spectre of an old lady was often seen sitting in a chair in one corner. She would appear and disappear regularly, although nobody was ever seen to enter or leave the room. Because the cleaners worked after everyone else in the building had gone home, the appearance of the spectre was not a tale which everyone employed there knew of.

Late one evening when most of the staff had gone home, Mr Ackril was asked by his colleague to take a file to the Director's office. Both men were in the basement at the time, and there had been a power-cut plunging the whole building into darkness. Mr Ackril was wary of going to the third floor alone in the dark, although he did not at the time know why this should be so. When his colleague refused to accompany him, although he had no idea why, Mr Ackril had no alternative but to take the file on his own up three flights of stairs in total darkness. It was only on his return downstairs that he was told by his colleague that he would not enter that room because he too had seen the apparition of the old lady! Although Mr Ackril had seen nothing in the Director's office that night, he later swore that if he had known the tale, then he would have left the file in the basement!

The Face at the Window

William Ward lost his daughter, aged twelve, to meningitis. Although this was many years ago, he recently heard, via a friend, from the people who now live in the house which he and his family had shared before his daughter's death. The family know nothing of this very personal tragedy, but have repeatedly seen the appearance of a ghostly face at the window. It is of a young girl around twelve years old, who seems to be staring into the kitchen, but never enters the house. Her description matches that of Mr Ward's daughter who died many years previously. Despite this, Mr Ward has never returned to the house, and feels that it would be unfair of him to inform the family concerned who the mystery face could be. He is convinced that it is his daughter.

A Ghostly Warning

Mr Eric Brotherton, an ex-collier from Dinnington, related the following account of a visit from beyond the grave...

Mr Brotherton's mother had been dead for a long while, when, several years ago, she appeared in a chair by his bed one morning as he awoke. She was looking down at him as he lay, and although no verbal communication passed from one to the other, he felt that he was being warned about something which was going to happen. Although Mr Brotherton's mother had died at a ripe old age, he described her appearance as much younger, in her prime. She was wearing a long dress and a large hat of the type which would have been in fashion when she was young. The apparition disappeared, but, aware that it embodied some sort of a warning, Mr Brotherton went about his business cautiously for the next few days. The following week, after a long-standing wrangle at work during which he feared that he was going to be used as a scapegoat, he lost his job. It was at this point that Mr Brotherton felt sure that his mother had indeed come to warn him beforehand. She has never appeared to him since.

It is not unusual for apparitions of long-dead people to appear as they would have done at the prime of life, rather than as they looked at the time of their dying. In this case, the lady in question also wore Victorian costume, although she had lived until the middle of this century.

Several other friends have appeared to Eric Brotherton throughout his life, each of whom he found out shortly afterwards had died on the very day they 'visited' him. In most cases, their apparitions stood at the end of his bed as he awoke, rather like portrait photographs in appearance. His most recent visitation occurred in 1994 when his father tried to communicate with him. However, the words he spoke were so unclear that Mr Brotherton could not understand the message that he evidently wanted to pass on.

A Family Connection

William Beldon Ward was the only boy-child born into his family, having four female cousins. Afraid that his family name would die when the girls married, his uncle requested that the young boy took his name. Consequently, 'Beldon' was added by the boy's parents, and William remained close to this branch of the family.

The two families lived a matter of doors away from each other, and socialised often. One night, in his childhood, William was woken by his favourite uncle who sat at the end of the bed and began to chat to him as he often did. They had been conversing for some time, when his father burst into the room. 'Who have you been speaking to?' he demanded, since he had been woken in the small hours by his young son's voice. 'Uncle Bill,' replied William innocently. His father then ran out of the house, jumped over the hedge and headed quickly in the direction of Bill's house... to find him dead in his chair. The child had no idea that he had been speaking to a spirit, but his father had realised instantly that something was wrong. Perhaps the dead man appeared to his namesake intentionally, viewing him as the son he never had. Indeed, at the reading of the Will, the boy found that he had been left his uncle's precious ring.

Lindholme Billy

A major fertiliser company uses the peaty soil on Hatfield Moor, Doncaster, in its gardening products. Workmen from the company have been digging here with heavy machinery for several years. A

Rotherham-based welding specialist, who has worked alongside the regular employees, remembers being told of strange sightings which occurred on the moor on a regular basis. The men use small vehicles to travel between sites, and on numerous occasions, the spectre of a man in pilot's uniform would appear as they were driving over a particular plot of land. The welder occasionally worked on this site himself, and although he never saw anything unusual, he recalls feeling uncomfortable when alone in the area.

In the late 1980's, one of the digging machines unearthed the body of a man on this very site. Peat is well known for its preservative qualities, and the body still wore garments identifiable as dated flying clothes. However, there were no clear markings on his uniform, nor did any buttons or 'dog tags' exist which would have helped the investigators to identify the body. Consequently, their find became known as 'Lindholme Billy' or 'Lindholme Willy'. A full-scale funeral for the assumed war casualty was announced. Many local people attended the unknown man's service as a mark of respect. Such an unusual event became well publicised, and television crews and reporters followed the story. Strangely, after the discovery of the body on Hatfield moor, and its subsequent lying to rest, sightings of the phantom airman ceased. Perhaps this was indeed another case of a restless spirit trying to attract attention to his plight, until he was finally discovered and buried in peace.

South Anston

In South Anston, there is an old path, or 'gennel', which leads to a row of cottages which have been standing for over two hundred years. One of these cottages needed renovation work in the early 1990's. A team of builders was busy at work one day when an old local man stopped to stare by the garden wall. "I wouldn't buy that house for love nor money," he said with a shake of his head, before walking off. None of the builders knew his name or why he had stopped to comment, although they remembered what he had said and told the new owner. However, the owner himself had no plans to live in the house, hoping instead to rent out the rooms separately to private tenants.

When the renovations were completed, the first tenants moved in and despite the house being difficult to heat because of its old stone floors, all went well. Then one day, one of the girls arrived downstairs in the morning to see an old man hanging a pair of curtains in the front room. She thought that he must be a friend of the landlord, and called a greeting. Only when she came out of the kitchen a few minutes later, and the man had vanished, did she realise that he could not possibly have left the house without passing her. Another tenant reported seeing an old man with a pipe sitting on the settee one afternoon, and before he 'disappeared', she had a clear enough description of his clothing to identify him as the same man seen by her flatmate. The smell of pipe smoke was often detected in the living room, despite none of the tenants smoking.

The turnover of tenants was very high at the cottage, and soon all the original occupiers had moved out. The landlord was not concerned, however, as more people filled the empty rooms as soon as they were advertised. The new tenants were unaware of the previous sightings in the house at this time. Within days of their moving in, they became aware of a strange atmosphere and the constant coldness of the place. It was as though the house carried an air of depression with it, which affected those who stayed there too long, and again several of the tenants moved out.

A carriage clock which was in the lounge had a habit of stopping and starting at will. The uncanny thing was, nobody ever re-set it, and yet it seemed to start on its own at the correct time, often after not having worked for several days. The tenants had no idea who the clock had originally belonged to, as it had been there since they moved in.

Two of the tenants were sitting in the large bedroom at the back of the house one night. The wall light and the bedside lamp were both on, when suddenly the wall lamp flicked off. Both men turned to look at it, and watched in amazement as the light bulb unscrewed itself and fell out of its previously secure socket!

By this time, the landlord himself had decided to move in, and took one of the vacant rooms. It did not take him long to feel that his house had a bad atmosphere, and the most frightening thing seemed to be that everyone who stayed there had experienced bad luck of one kind or another. The house only remained occupied for a further three months. The landlord and tenants moved out, and repeated attempts to sell the place failed.

Many years ago, a man is said to have gassed himself in the kitchen. Two of the early tenants reported having had suicidal feelings while lodging there, although at the time they could find no reason for the sudden surge of depression which overtook them, yet today, this beautiful cottage may have new tenants, who are untouched by its troubled past...

Drawn by R.Hobbard Esq.   Engraved by J Bodon.

CHURCH OF LAUGHTON EN LE MORTHING.

The churches of South Anston and Laughton share many architectural features. *See p. 101.*

"The face of the spectre was not visible, and it appeared to be gliding at great speed in their direction..."

HISTORIC SITES AND HAUNTED HALLS

The following historic sites and buildings are situated in and around South Yorkshire. Much of their history pre-dates Domesday, but since folklore persists, the oldest ghosts continue to walk alongside the more modern ones...

Mosborough Hall Hotel

Many years ago, the terrain around the Mosborough area of Sheffield was an expanse of unbroken moorland. This is reflected in the origin of its name, as Mosborough is an adaptation of 'Moresburgh', which means 'The fort on the moor'. Today, this statuesque Hotel can be found just outside Sheffield, on the A616 towards Chesterfield.

The Saxon Wulfric Spott, who owned lands as far as Conisborough in Doncaster and Laughton in Rotherham in Ethelred's reign, was also over-lord of Mosborough at the end of the 10th century. Twenty years after the Norman Conquest, Mosborough was passed on to its new Norman lord, Ralph Fitzhubert. Fitzhubert and Roger di Busli were two of the major South Yorkshire land-holders after the Conquest. However, rather than implying that Fitzhubert had taken up residence in his newly-won lands, he possibly rarely ever visited Mosborough! Noble landlords were often absentees, spending much of their time at court or abroad, although the existence of a fort in Mosborough would suggest that a household of importance was in residence at some point in history.

The Hall itself has features in common with many historic houses, in that it has been a site for continual re-building and updating. Hence, nobody can be quite sure of the date of the first Hall, although it could have been built as long ago as Saxon times. Much of the current building is 17th century in origin.

81

Mosborough Hall has seen many owners throughout history, and was even commandeered during the Civil War in the 17th century. According to the history leaflet supplied by the current owners (who purchased the building in 1974), Cyril Wells, the local colliery owner, bought Mosborough Hall in the 1930's. One of the most popular stories associated with Mosborough Hall is that of a young woman who was murdered here many years ago. Her lover is said to have stabbed her to death in a midnight row, and ever since, her ghost has walked the house and grounds on certain nights of the year.

According to Mr Sam Beecher, manager at Mosborough Hall, an apparition has been seen by staff and visitors on many occasions, and appears on average up to four times a year. Mr Nicholas, the co-manager of the Hall, now logs all sightings of their mysterious guest as and when they are reported! Each time a room has been renovated and its structure altered (such as removal of walls and floorboards and so on), the ghost is reputed to show her distress.

Receptionist Jean Macmillan was sitting in the bar one afternoon when she saw the figure of a woman gliding through the dining area, wearing a long grey high-bodiced dress with white collar and cuffs, and floor-length pleats. The figure's dark hair was taken back into a bun, although Miss Macmillan could not see her face. The spectre appeared by the window in the restaurant, and headed towards the bottom end of the dining room where there had once been a passage. The lady seated next to Miss Macmillan at the time also saw 'something', probably the end of the woman's trailing dress, although she could not be as specific in her description. The following week, a visitor to Mosborough Hall was sitting in the bar when he too saw the woman in the dining room! More recently, Miss Macmillan was able to identify the costume the grey lady wore as that of the Georgian period.

One of the male guests recounted seeing a woman appear in his room one night, as his wife slept beside him. He was so taken by her beauty that he did not wake his wife, and continued to watch the apparition in fascination!

The following story was recounted by the granddaughter of a lady who worked as the cook at Mosborough Hall, until her marriage in 1901 when she left domestic service. Mr Beecher feels that the room described in this particular account is most likely to be the current Room 22, which was number 9 until a recent extension was added.

The Hall was known to be haunted in the 1800's by the family who resided there. There were many strange happenings in the house, but the most spectacular of these was centred on a room which is believed to have once been the library, although later became a bedroom. This particular room was plagued by a poltergeist. Ornaments and books were thrown around and furniture was moved from one side of the room to the other almost every day. At first, residents of the Hall were blamed; in those days, all domestic staff who were employed had their own quarters in the building, and a great number were needed to run a house of such size. However, many of the staff were afraid to go into the room, and the Squire became concerned about their tales.

In an attempt to discover whether there was indeed anything amiss, or whether a sinister joker on his staff was to blame, he devised a plan. One day, he sealed the library to all outside visitors. Each one of the windows, every door, and every possible route by which a person could enter or leave the room was dealt with. However, the Squire decided prudently that he would not spend a night in the room alone; he opted to sleep outside the main door, which he locked before laying down on his mattress. Whether or not the Squire was woken in the middle of the night by strange goings on from inside the room, or even if he managed to sleep at all, is unknown. However, in the morning the door was unlocked to reveal furniture, books and ornaments scattered all over as they had been many times before...

Whether or not the phantom of the murdered woman was responsible for the happenings at the end of the 19th century, or if indeed she is the Grey Lady currently in residence, is unclear... but it is conceivable that a building with such a history as Mosborough Hall might have more than one ghost!

Dinnington Barrow

In 1862 a Barrow was discovered and excavated close to Park Avenue Road in the small ex-colliery town of Dinnington, twelve miles outside Sheffield. Dr Rolleston, a local archaeologist who worked in the Oxford Museum at the time, returned home to supervise the proceedings. The barrow was 8 feet high and 42 yards long, and contained over twenty skeletons of people of all ages and both sexes. Most were buried in a crouching position, but one figure was laid out with the head pointing North, and another was unearthed in the southern end of the burial chamber. The remains varied in depth, some being twenty feet deep and others only two feet below the surface.

The lack of artefacts in the burial mound itself led Dr Rolleston to believe that the barrow was very old indeed. Barrow burials ceased around the time Christianity became the predominant religion, which was approximately 627 AD. The skulls were of the elongated Neolithic type, and further investigation concluded that they belonged to people of the New Stone Age. This would mean that Dinnington was inhabited over four thousand years ago by the people who constructed the burial chamber. The skulls were originally placed in the Oxford Museum, but Clifton in Rotherham now holds many of the artefacts unearthed here.

In the late 1970's and early 1980's, many new houses were constructed around the site. The barrow area itself was shrouded in woodland, and several of the new residents reported seeing ghostly white figures wandering between the trees at night. Perhaps the digging of what was once hallowed ground had disturbed the sleeping spirits of the old barrow; there is still a strange atmosphere in this area today, and only the daring will walk their dogs here after dark.

Old Thorpe Hall
See p. 95

Dinnington Hall

In Saxon times, the village green of the settlement at Dinnington was close to what is now the Falcon Inn. There are still the remains of an ancient wall of Saxon origin near to St Leonard's Church. In these times, the village was known as the 'Tun of Dynne's People', although nobody can be sure as to the exact identity of Dynne. The Falcon took its name from a member of the local Athorpe family who was Chief Falconer to James I, and kept his hawks near the Church. The Athorpes were the last landowners to hold the Hall at Dinnington, and today their crest of a hawk is still used by Dinnington Comprehensive School as a housebase motif.

Many of the surviving cottages in this area were originally servants' houses and farm outbuildings belonging to the original estate, which was managed from Dinnington Hall. The original Old Hall is now the farmhouse on Laughton Road, and is thought to be the oldest surviving building in the village. The modern Hall was built in 1756 by Henry Athorpe. When his nephew Robert inherited, it was considerably smaller, and many extra rooms were added in the 1800's.

Over the years, the outbuildings were sold off for private residence, and several were converted. The house which today is number 2, opposite Dean's Restaurant, was once two separate buildings: a coaching house, and servants' quarters. In the early part of the century a wall was knocked down to allow more spacious living accommodation for the new tenants. Pat Dean, an ex-Dinnington collier who now lives in North Anston, grew up in this house, and related a strange experience from his childhood. One night while lying in bed awake, as a teenager, he was looking out onto the landing when a figure appeared from nowhere and walked into the bedroom. It was the spectre of a tall man wearing a long pale cloak and a top hat with a feather in it. The apparition was solid enough for Mr Dean to see the face and body of the man in detail, although he could not see its feet. Instantly he panicked and called out, at which point lights came on throughout the house and the vision disappeared.

On other occasions, the family dog would lift its head as though watching something go by, which was invisible to the human eyes in the room. An old mantelpiece clock, which had not worked for many years, was strangely working again one morning when the family came down to breakfast, although nobody could find any reason for this to be so.

Some years later, while in Worksop, Mr Dean visited the town library and saw an identical outfit, of long pale cape and top hat with a feather, which was the uniform worn by the local 19th century coachman. In a book written by local historian Mrs J Drinkwater, there is a series of photographs taken at the time Dinnington Hall was still being run as a household. In one of these, the staff of the Hall are grouped together for a portrait. In the centre is the coachman, a Mr Jackson, whom Mr Dean immediately recognised as the man who had walked into his bedroom several years earlier. Number 2 is still owned today by members of the Dean family, who occasionally feel strange presences in the house, although no further sightings have occurred.

The Green Lady of Throapham

The old Manor House at the hamlet of Throapham, near Dinnington, was demolished earlier this century. All that now remains of the structure, which was last owned by the Skinner family, is piles of bricks and tiles, and an avenue of old yew trees. At one time, Throapham Manor was a focal point for local fox hunts, and even boasted its own special breed of heavy horses which were used for working in the fields. The Manor had bee hives, an orchard, and a 'pinfold' - a pen for stray animals which was of Medieval origin. Many old residents of Throapham and the surrounding villages remember the ghost of the Green Lady. She is said to walk from the site of the Manor house down a path to the orchard at a certain time of year, and then disappear. Even after the Manor was demolished the Green Lady continued her walk, and for the pupils at Dinnington Comprehensive School, who still run their cross-country course through Throapham wood, the stories are a constant source of fear.

Aston Hall Hotel

On the outskirts of Sheffield, heading towards the North Nottinghamshire border on Worksop Road, sits a fine 18th century Hall which was designed by renowned architect John Carr. Originally, a much older house had occupied the same site. The structure of the Hall was continually being altered and added to until 1825, and today, Aston Hall is a magnificent hotel featuring an original mosaic floor in the reception.

The guide leaflet issued at the Hall describes rumours of a famous romance said to have taken place here:

'Aston Hall was once visited by the two Lord Byrons, father and son, on different occasions and both are rumoured to have run off with the Lady of the Manor. The father apparently went to Paris with his lover but his son, the famous poet, only took his lover to Newstead Abbey where he changed his mind and sent his lady friend back to Aston Hall.'

The guide goes on to suggest that several murders took place here in its early days. There are also tales of a secret passage which is said to run from one of the bedrooms.

Although none of the current staff are aware of having seen or felt anything unusual in their workplace, the following account was given by a long-time Aston resident who does not wish to be named. When this lady was a child, she would visit a Mrs Levick, who had once been a lady's maid at Aston Hall. Mrs Levick knew of one of the darker legends of the Hall, in which many years ago the lady of the house, Lady Pagett, is rumoured to have fallen in love with a butler who murdered her at a secret tryst in an underground tunnel, which ran from the old white house in Aston to Aughton Hall. Mrs Levick was not the only one who knew of the story. The lady who recounted this tale was also told by her grandmother and other relatives (who lived in an Aston cottage over the site of the tunnel) that a woman's screams and running footsteps had been heard emanating from 'underground' at certain times of the year. Indeed, in those days, the subterranean tunnel was under fields close to their back garden. If Lady Pagett had indulged in such an affair, then her family would quite naturally have tried to silence gossip by closing ranks and attempting to cover the matter up. If her spirit still wanders underground reliving the moment of her murder, nobody has recently reported hearing her cries.

Interestingly, the white house which is reputed to be linked to the tunnel remained empty and dilapidated for many years, and was rumoured to be haunted in its own right.

Another story was put forward by a recent visitor to the Hall, carpenter Robert Lenton. In 1992, a friend of Mr Lenton's who worked at the Hotel invited him to have a look around. She recounted how one of the bedrooms was supposedly haunted by a presence which made itself felt from time to time. The room would suddenly become freezing cold, and the curtains would billow as though being blown by a breeze... even when the windows were closed and the weather outside was fair and warm. Allegedly, visitors who spent the night in this room would complain of their discomfort the morning after, and refuse to be housed there again. It is now supposedly disused. Although Mr Lenton did not visit this room, he did go down into the cellar. He was told that the Hall had once been a mental institution, and a certain cellar room had been used to prepare the bodies of any who had died there. This room was of bare stone, with channels cut around the base of the walls, and contained an enormous stone slab which had been used to 'lay out' the dead. Mr Lenton felt that the atmosphere was chilled and unpleasant, and left the cellar quickly!

The Todwick Highwayman

Todwick, close to the M1 motorway approximately ten miles from Sheffield, is a picturesque agricultural village sporting many fine old farm buildings. The following story was recounted by a local woman who travels home through the village, and on one occasion was surprised by an unexpected fellow traveller...

Late one night just before Christmas in the late 1980's, Vinty Ackril was driving home from an office Christmas party which had been held in Sheffield. Although it was late, she was not particularly tired, and had not been drinking due to the fact that she had to drive home. It was around midnight as she turned left at Todwick crossroads next to The Red Lion Hotel, on to Dinnington Lane. There are few lights and many overhanging trees in this area, and old earth banks, which traditionally marked the boundaries between fields, can still be seen. Miss Ackril was taken by surprise when a dark shape appeared directly in front of her car and was illuminated by the headlights. It was the figure of a man sitting on a dark horse, wearing a long flowing cape which was spread out over the horse's rump. He had a strangely shaped hat with a peak at the front, which Miss Ackril identified as one of the old tricorn type. The horse and rider darted in front of the car and disappeared over one of the hedges and into the adjoining field. Miss Ackril instantly knew that she had seen the apparition of a highwayman, but felt more surprised than frightened.

The following day, in an attempt to rule out any 'rational' explanation for the sighting, she drove to Dinnington Lane in the daylight. At the very spot where the highwayman had appeared, she stopped the car to look at the surrounding area. However, there were no overhanging boughs or other natural features in the landscape which could have possibly made her believe that a highwayman had ridden out in front of her the night before.

North and South Anston

North and South Anston are divided by the main A57 Worksop road, approximately twelve miles from Sheffield. The name 'Anston' is said to stem from a word meaning 'One Stone', although whether this indicates an ancient landmark or just an area of good quarrying stone, nobody is sure. Both villages have their own interesting history, despite being little heard of by those who live closer to the city of Sheffield.

The remains of a Stone Age settlement have been unearthed at Anston Stones, which is now a protected area of green belt land. Dead Man's Cave, deep in the heart of the Stones, revealed artefacts which suggested that the area was possibly a Stone Age hunting outpost from Cresswell Craggs. Thousands of years later, Anston was recorded in Domesday as a small farming hamlet. Indeed, it continued as a tiny agricultural community until the sinking of Dinnington Colliery in the early 20th century.

Certain areas of woodland in the Stones have their own peculiar atmosphere. Many ancient groves of trees, particularly yew, are found in the heart of these woods. Although local people walk their dogs around here, there are certain places by the old railway line (still in use for coal transportation) which are full of darkness and foreboding. Fewer people use these walks. Several years ago, a group of schoolboys decided to camp out for the night in one of the many grassy clearings. They were terrified by the sight of an illuminated figure which shone with a bluish light, standing underneath an old oak tree. Rather than continue with their camping adventure, they rode home on their bikes as fast as they could!

Local folklore tells how the Palace of Westminster and the main Record Office in London were built from stone mined at Anston quarries, being some of the finest for many miles around. Two government commissioners were riding from Nottingham to Newark when they espied Southwell Minster, in Nottinghamshire, lit by a beautiful sunset. They enquired as to where the stone which built the Minster had come from, and were told Anston. They reported this on their return to London, and it was agreed that Anston stone should indeed be used in London. The quarried stone had to be taken by barge from the Chesterfield Canal to the wharf at Kiveton Bridge, where it was transported up the River Trent, down the Humber, and round the coast to the Thames. Even today, many of the old local surnames of Anston inhabitants show that quarrying and stonemasonry were once principal crafts in the area.

In the middle of the 1960's Orchard Avenue and The Oval were built on top of what local legend says is a Saxon burial ground. The Bakers have lived on Orchard Avenue since the houses were built in 1963. For over thirty years there have been sounds of an unseen visitor pacing up and down the stairs, at all times of the day and night. Members of the family often hear footsteps and assume that somebody is coming up or down the stairs, but on further investigation, find nobody there. Once, a 'cold spot' was found in one corner of the living-room, which could be stepped in and out of at will, making the hairs on the back of the neck stand on end. It disappeared after about half an hour, but has not been experienced since. Family friends have also heard the phantom footsteps, although these no longer frighten the residents, who refer to their unseen visitor as 'Henry'.

When the houses on The Oval were first being constructed, builders went into one particular bungalow to concrete a floor. They finished in the late afternoon and locked up as normal. However, they returned the next morning to find footsteps imprinted in the dried concrete, and further investigation indicated that these belonged to sandalled feet, although the house had been locked all night and there was no way that anybody could have found entry to the room.

Butcher's Orchard, next to the old Roman Wells, has its own grue-some tale. The field covered with tall weeds and shrubs was said to have been the site of a great battle between the Norman invaders and the Saxon land-holders. During the battle, so many men were killed that the ground ran red with their blood, hence the name 'butcher's orchard', which has survived until this day. A recent building operation on the land was said to be ill-omened; it was felt that the houses would never sell, although how much of this is due to local folklore and how much will prove to be true is another matter.

St James' Church is a landmark for miles around, being situated on an ancient hill at the top of South Anston, visible from the A57 Work-sop. The junction is traditionally known as Paradise Square since the famous hymn-writer John Wesley arrived in Anston to preach.

The building of the Church as it now stands was begun around 1174, although an earlier Saxon church is believed to have stood here. One of the interior walls shows the remains of an older building, now incorporated into the tower. According to local researchers from the Workers Educational Association, a flagstone carved with a Saxon wheel cross was found in the 1800's, although this was destroyed later in the same century.

The following strange tale was related by Mr John Ireland, the local Conservative councillor. During the mid-'80s, on a Sunday evening, the service was being conducted by a deputy for the resident vicar, who was on holiday. The processional song was over and the opening prayers were given. The vicar announced 'We will now sing the Magnificat', and as normal, the organist struck up his first chord and the choir, nine or so women and children, rose from their stalls. On the wall next to the choir were two commemorative plaques, three feet high and over four feet wide, which were pinned to the wall with steel pins due to their extreme weight. One of these plaques was also on two large stone feet approximately five feet above the height of the floor. At the very point the choir rose, this particular plaque crashed from the wall and fell straight into the stalls, shattering.

Miraculously, not one person from the choir itself was hurt, despite a large pile of rubble landing in the very area the children occupied. Pieces of the shattered plaque bounced through the congregation injuring the Choirmaster and a local farmer, who needed immediate medical attention. Only later was it discovered that the enormous church clock at the top of the tower had stopped at exactly twenty to seven, ten minutes after the evening service had begun, and the exact time that the plaque had crashed from the wall.

The Church was closed for nearly a month while teams of surveyors investigated the building to make sure that the structure was safe. No reason for the 'accident' was ever found. The tower clock was re-balanced and St James' was eventually reopened. Sceptics prefer the explanation that a tremor from the local Axle coal-fault was to blame for the strange happenings, shaking the plaque from the wall and vibrating the tower so that the clock stopped. However, if this was the case, it is surprising that no other damage was recorded elsewhere in the village... and that a plaque secured by steel pins somehow took the impact and stopped the church clock!

Roche Abbey

Roche Abbey, in the district of Maltby, Rotherham, was founded in 1147 by a Cistercian brotherhood who had travelled down from Newminster Abbey at Northumberland. Although they arrived in the valley in 1140, for several years they lived without a proper dwelling until the local lords offered to build them an abbey. 'Roche' means 'rock', and popular folklore has it that a vision of the crucifix appeared on a certain rock close by and inspired the monks to settle here.

The Abbey was originally known as the Abbey of Santa Maria de Rupe. Although it has been said that no dead were ever buried at Roche Abbey (and that instead they were carried to Blythe Priory to be interred) Les Halford, employed in the Abbey House, explained that this is not strictly true. There is a small number of graves belonging to local landowners who bequeathed money to the Abbey in their lifetime, on the condition that, after their deaths, the monks would pray for their souls.

Around 1534, Henry VIII ordered an investigation into all monasteries in England prior to their Dissolution. The Abbey was visited by the feared Doctors Leigh and Layton, who had the task of presenting a 'black book' of their findings to the King. Although Roche Abbey escaped closure at first, being found to be financially viable, on their second visit in 1537, Leigh and Layton reported that 'Two thirds of all monks in England were drunkards and so bad as to defy description' and the Abbey was closed. According to all surviving documentation, there was no massacre at the Abbey; the monks were pensioned off peaceably but still tried frantically to hide their pewter chalices in the woods, while the local people took hymn books and pews to repair their carts and wagons! It was also said in the report by Leigh and Layton that the monks worshipped a nearby rock on which there was an image of the crucifix. Perhaps this recalls the legend of why the site for Roche Abbey was selected in the first place.

If such a rock still survives, it must be deeply buried in the woodland which surrounds the ruins. Indeed, there are many ancient yew trees whose age must number hundreds of years in the surrounding grounds. Yews are often associated with worship groves of the pre-Christian religion; it is not hard to imagine that the area around Roche Abbey has been sacred for longer than there has been a Christian monastery standing.

The Abbey House is only 240 years old, although it appears much older. It was originally built as a hunting and gaming lodge for the well-to-do. Many local people have taken stones in the past from the ruined Abbey to build their houses, and it is possible that much of the stone used to build the Abbey House is from the Abbey itself.

According to Mr Halford, there are stories from local people who have walked around the Abbey at dusk, and seen the spectre of a grey lady standing at one of the windows, staring out onto the grounds. The sound of a wailing child is said to be heard coming from one of the upper rooms, although on investigation the crying stops and the room is empty. Certain guests are also said to have seen the ghost of a maid disappearing up a flight of stairs. Legend has it that in the 18th century, a maidservant had found herself pregnant, and shortly after her child was born, she killed the baby before hanging herself in the attic.

On New Year's morning in 1991, four local people reported seeing the spectre of a figure clad in white robes, heading across the grass behind the gatehouse towards them. The Cistercian order who founded the monastery did indeed wear white robes all year round, having no change of clothes or extra garments throughout the seasons. The face of the spectre was not visible, and it appeared to be gliding at a great speed in their direction, glowing with an unearthly greyish light. The area of grass it walked over was once the site of the wooden buildings which temporarily housed the monks and their Abbey guests, until the stone structure was built.

Later that same year, at about nine o' clock at night, the same group of friends were waiting in the small car park below the steep crags which surround one side of the valley. Noises so strange and unearthly were emanating from the trees above them that they became afraid to get out of the car, despite having walked around the grounds many times before at later hours than this. The source of the noises proved impossible to locate, and the group left in fear.

Indeed, the atmosphere around the Abbey is reputed to change from day to day; sometimes it is peaceful and calm, and at others, so menacing that it defies those who wish to enter.

Towards the far end of the Abbey itself, there lies a small stone coffin without a lid. Local legend has it that if one is to stare for long enough at the head of the coffin, then a face will appear, although nobody is sure of its origins. Why the coffin was never used remains a mystery.

Old monasteries and historic houses are often associated with secret underground tunnels and 'priest holes', places in which to conceal the people who lived within. In times of religious uncertainty, when popes and abbots often opposed each other and the affairs of God were entangled with the affairs of state, the enclosed order was not always a safe one. Even before the Church was split into the opposing factions of Catholic and Protestant, many preachers were arrested and accused of heresy for their beliefs. A quick escape route was felt to be the safest policy, and Roche Abbey was no exception to this. There is a network of underground tunnels beneath the abbey, leading to Houses and Castles of consequence. Some of the tunnels run for miles, and have only been blocked for safety reasons within the last few years.

The Thorpe Salvin Highwayman

In the Rotherham area of the old West Riding of Yorkshire there still exists an intriguing network of ancient lanes, which lead between little-visited villages such as Gildingwells, Thorpe Salvin, Stone and Firbeck, to name but a few. Any of these historic stone-built places is well worth a visit for keen walkers and picnickers, throughout the summer months. They are surprisingly easy to locate, via the A57 or the A634 roads.

Many of the old lanes mark ancient trade routes which have been used since Roman times, the most renowned of which is Packman Lane. Another such road which leads to Thorpe Salvin (and is still surrounded by fields and the old traditional hawthorn hedges and banks) holds an interesting secret to which many local people can testify. At a certain point in this lane, there is a small dip in the contour of the land. When cars drive down into the dip at night, their headlights for a second seem to illuminate something strange at the top of the hill. There have been several reports of the flash of a silver stirrup and more sightings of a man on a black horse hailing the vehicles that pass. He is dressed in a dark cape and an old-fashioned hat, and his face is covered. As soon as the vehicle headlights shine away from the figure, it can no longer be seen. In 1991 a group of friends saw the spectre and decided to turn their car around and try to spot it again. They drove backwards and forwards no fewer than five times, and each time the figure was seen appearing from the same place at the side of the road and vanishing again as the car advanced up the hill. The highwayman's ghost seems to be triggered by the approach of vehicles and lights: cars are, after all, the modern version of the old stagecoaches which he must have robbed in the still of the night.

Local legend suggests that a highwayman was caught near here and hanged, his body being left to rot on a gibbet close to the old village border of Thorpe Salvin, where he had laid in wait for unwitting travellers during his notorious career. Although nobody can be sure how true this is, it was certainly a common practice until the 1800's to leave a criminal's body in a gibbet at a boundary wall, to warn others of the consequences of breaking the law.

Thorpe Salvin

Thorpe Salvin is a historic village a short distance from the North Nottinghamshire border, boasting the ruins of an Elizabethan square-style manor. Thorpe Hall was once a quadrangular house with circular turrets at each corner. In two of these turrets, which are still visible today, there were winding staircases, and a main through-hall divided the house into two main halves.

The village of Thorpe Salvin is separated from Harthill by an old road of which the early 19th century historian, Joseph Hunter, noted: 'The western boundary of Thorpe-Salvin is the antient highway, now called Packman's Lane, but antiently the Street.' This is believed to be of Roman origin, due to its straight course towards the passage over the River Don, and the village's Medieval name of Rykenild-thorpe. Rykenild was the name given to many Roman roads. Roman coins have also been found locally, and the apparition of a Roman legion is said to walk along the road from time to time!

The Salvins were one of the earliest recorded families in the village, and their name began to be used in preference to the earlier Rykenild-thorpe. In Elizabethan times the land passed into the Sandford family, and the Old Hall as we see it today was built. Tragically, within a few years of its completion, the Lord of the manor, Henry Sandford, died leaving three daughters too young to inherit. Although two of them, Helen and Elizabeth, did reside here at some point later in their lives, the building was eventually sold to the Osbornes. From here on, Thorpe Hall was only ever used as an occasional residence.

There are stories of a mystery figure which has been seen walking in between the empty windows of the remaining walls. A silhouette is said to appear on a brick outcrop in the light of the moon. When viewed from the road at night, the building appears at first glance to be an entire Manor until you step closer to look and find only the front wall intact. It seems that no family was ever comfortable here for long, and within a short space of time the building fell into ruins.

Despite its size and seeming inconsequentiality, Thorpe Salvin did not escape the conflict of Civil War in the 17th century. In the Parish register it is noted that 'There were five men buried in the beginninge of October, being slain in a fight on Thorpe more between the garrison of Welbeck on the King's part and Captain Rodes on the Parlament part. An. Do. 1645.'

A garrison of Parliamentarians was based near Worksop. In a skirmish with the Welbeck Royalists, who had drawn some of their number from Thorpe Salvin, the Parliamentarians killed two men. Major John Jametz planned a retaliation attack on behalf of the Royalists, only to find that he and his men were heavily outnumbered. By then it was too late to retreat; five men were killed and forty were taken prisoner. One man escaped, Thomas Battersbie, whose hand they had severed. It was buried in the Churchyard at Thorpe Salvin, and later gave rise to the rumours of a phantom disembodied hand.

The Green Lady of Firbeck Hall

Firbeck took its name from 'Frith Beck', meaning 'the stream in the woodland'. The stream in question is one which runs through Roche Abbey, and supplied the monastery and early local villages with fresh water. Over the centuries, 'Frith Beck' became 'Firthbeck', and eventually Firbeck. It is today a picturesque village in Rotherham.

Firbeck Hall was used as a mining rehabilitation centre after the war, and dealt with serious pit accident cases. Today it stands empty, although there has been local concern about current plans proposed for its use. It was once the haunt of the old Prince of Wales, who later married the divorcée Wallis Simpson and became the Duke of Windsor. Before his marriage and consequent abdication, the Prince would often take weekend breaks in Firbeck, which became one of his many country hideaways. What could have been more ideal than escaping from his public duties to a little Northern village with a small population? Mrs Clarice Chadderton was a Land Girl in Firbeck Hall grounds during the Second World War, and remembers how the Prince's small biplane could be seen flying over the fields as he prepared to touch down. Many of the locals hoped to catch a glimpse of him, but the hall is secluded, and only those who worked in and around it were privileged enough to see him.

Firbeck Hall has its own beautiful grounds, containing a small lake. Many years ago a young woman fell in to the lake and drowned. Whether she was a daughter of the house, a servant, or one of the villagers is not known. In the early days of Firbeck Colliery, many of the miners would walk past the Hall after finishing on night duty hoping to hear the nightingales sing on their way home. On certain nights of the year, some of them said they had seen the spectre of a Green Lady appear from her watery grave and walk out to shore in her dripping clothes.

The Schire Oakes

Shireoaks is a small North Nottinghamshire village on three county borders - those of Nottinghamshire, Derbyshire and Yorkshire. In Medieval times, landmarks such as groves of large old trees were used to mark boundaries on the land, much as we have sign posts today. The village of Shireoaks takes its name from such a grove, although the border lines have changed by a mile or two these days. Oak trees are held with a particular kind of reverence in folklore, probably stemming from the days when Druids were associated with sacred oak groves. It is said that their pagan worship took place under such trees, which were used as meeting places. None of the original medieval oaks still stand in Shireoaks today, although there are cases elsewhere of their having survived for many hundreds of years (such as the Major Oak in Sherwood Forest). Was it possible that the original 'Schire Oakes' were once part of an ancient Druid Grove, saved from being torn out of the ground by the new Christian church because they came to mark three important border-lines? The three Shire borders which meet near this point have changed many times over the centuries, according to old maps, perhaps as the original trees disappeared. Did they indeed have a religious significance way back in history?

Tickhill

Modern Tickhill, near Doncaster, retains some the character of its historic past in the site of the old castle and the beautiful little lake, which is a legacy of the old moat. The name Tickhill is believed to have originated from 'Wick Hill'. 'Wick' is an ancient word used to describe a fortified mount, thought to have existed here since before the present 12th century castle was built. Before the Norman Conquest, the two major land-holders in Tickhill were the Saxons Elsi and Seward. No record of a major building exists in Saxon Tickhill, so when the Normans constructed the Castle, it was most likely on top of ancient earthworks which had existed for many years previously. As is often the case, a rise of land would be used for centuries by each conquering people who occupied it, being built and rebuilt as many times as was necessary. The Norman Roger di Busli undertook the construction of Tickhill Castle, which suggests that, of all the lands he had been awarded as the spoils of war, Tickhill was perhaps his true residing place in South Yorkshire.

Historian Joseph Hunter noted wryly that 'there are few facts connected with the conquest more extraordinary than the willingness which the Normans shewed to abandon their own country and to become settled inhabitants of ours.' Indeed, di Busli gave up his lands in Normandy with no intention of residing there again, following his move to Tickhill!

Sadly, many of the castle walls are today in disrepair, and 'Danger' notices warn curious visitors not to get too close. The tranquillity surrounding the current village must be a contrast to its busy, often violent history. Tickhill Castle housed garrisons of soldiers and their horses for hundreds of years; as late as the 17th century there are records of men from here being dispatched and captured in wartime England. The castle was the site of many sieges, not least of all in 1321 when the local constable, William de Anne, held out one winter for three weeks, being forced to live alongside the other occupants on badly-stored rations.

In the time of Richard I, royal tournaments were held in Tickhill. Henry II's queen, the French Eleanor of Aquitaine, founded a chapel to St Nicholas within the castle walls. Being part of a private estate, this is unfortunately not accessible to visitors. At the end of the 1300's, Catherine Swinford, the Duchess of Lancaster, took over custodianship of Tickhill Castle (along with Knaresborough) on her husband's death. Indeed, Tickhill was a Lancastrian stronghold for many years.

Other places of interest in Tickhill abound. The site of an ancient (possibly Saxon) church is remembered only as All Hallows field, which has revealed old gravestones to those who have searched there in the past. As long ago as 1664, this area was known as 'the church', although the building itself had disappeared much earlier. The eye-catching Butter Cross monument was built c. 1777 to replace the original

Medieval market cross. Local legend says that the original now stands at Wellingley Lane junction. The public footpath running past the castle is a must for visitors, and provides a wonderful walk for those who are interested in the area.

The Chesterfield Canal

During the Industrial Revolution, the businessmen of Chesterfield and Retford decided that local trade transport arrangements were no longer adequate. Packhorses were used to carry panniers of goods towards Bawtry, where a passage over the River Idle led to the Trent and hence to the east coast. Because only relatively small amounts of goods could be transported in this manner, it was decided that a canal was needed. Local canal enthusiast Mr Cliff Hodgetts is well-acquainted with the history of the Chesterfield Canal, and was able to supply details of its construction, from his own research.

Building began in May 1771, leading to 46 miles of waterway and 65 locks being constructed. The longest tunnel excavated was the major Norwood tunnel, which took three years to dig in its own right. At a length of 2,850 yards it was the longest tunnel for its period in the whole of Europe. The men responsible for the canal worked as close to the site as they could; they built kilns by its banks to bake more than two million bricks needed during construction. By June 1777, the canal had been completed. One of its more famous uses was shipping canon balls, which were cast in Chesterfield, to be used in the Napoleonic Wars. However, at one point in particular, the canal was not cut on a straight course. This is because an ancient plague-pit had been dug many years before, close to the village of Brimington in Derbyshire, which now appears as a mound in the land. The plague decimated whole communities, and individual burials were often impossible. Any number of bodies could be heaped into a communal grave such as this one, with no records of who they were or exactly when they died. These burial grounds were subsequently declared Hallowed Ground, and disturbing them is still to this day frowned upon. The course of the Chesterfield canal was forced to avoid the hallowed ground rather than cutting through it.

The following story was related by Arthur Skelhorn, a resident of Brimington. Mr Skelhorn had no idea that he was living close to such an ancient site when he recounted the following experience, which took place in the winter of 1993.

Mr Skelhorn has always walked his dog along the banks of the Chesterfield canal, twice daily. One cold evening as the dusk was setting in, he went out as normal despite being slightly later than he had intended. A mist had risen off of the water, and the air was chill. Not wanting to deprive his dog of its walk, Mr Skelhorn dutifully headed down Cow Lane and towards the canal bank. (It is at this point that the outcrop of land is formed, where the canal was not cut on a straight course.)

Mr Skelhorn noticed the very tall figure of a man, over six feet in height, wearing a long dark coat which trailed the floor, and a large top hat. The figure was standing approximately twenty feet in front of him. Mr Skelhorn remembers instantly becoming wary, although he rationalised that the man could be waiting to ask him for directions and so began to walk towards him. At this point, his dog, who normally runs towards strangers, did not leave his side.

The figure disappeared before Mr Skelhorn had reached it. He walked past the outcrop of land and round the corner in the hope of seeing where the man had gone, but the 150 yard straight towpath was completely empty. There was nobody on the embankment, and it was not possible for a man to have been standing on the outcrop and then disappear from sight in the time it took Mr Skelhorn to walk around the corner. When he arrived home, he assured his wife he would never go alone to that area of the canal again after dark. Indeed, it is an area which has often been described as eerie, even in the daytime. For many years it overgrown with weeds, and only recently has conservation work been undertaken to encourage its safe use by walkers and tourists.

In 1994, Mr Skelhorn heard from another Brimington resident whose son had seen a similar mystery figure in the 1970's. The boy was walking along a lane behind King Street with a friend, when a tall man in a long dark coat and a top hat stepped out of the shadows. The children ran home and reported what they had seen, in such distress that their mother recounted the description they gave quite clearly, despite the event happening over 20 years ago.

It would seem that the mystery man has been walking the banks of the Chesterfield Canal for longer than Mr Skelhorn imagined; perhaps there are more residents of Brimington who could add to the tale.

Laughton and The Gallows

In the Middle Ages, Laughton was a thriving market town which drew custom from the neighbouring Shires and surrounding villages. Its name is derived from the fact that it was a 'Law Town', and therefore a governing centre for the whole district. In the reign of the Saxon King Ethelred, Wolfric Spott was lord of Conisborough and held this land. The last Saxon lord to hold the estate was Edwin, who was forced to give way to Roger di Busli at the time of the conquest. Saxon Lords all over England were superseded by Normans who were granted lands by the Conqueror for their services.

Castle Hill, close to the ancient farm manor house near All Saints Church, was once the site of the great Laughton Castle. It is rumoured that the Empress Maud stayed here; if this is true, it points to the size and importance of Laughton as a fortified centre at the time.

The population of Laughton decreased at some point in history; today it is a small rural village centred around a farming community. One possible reason for this sudden demise could have been the onset of the plague. There were two types of plague which swept Europe in the Middle ages, one of which was the Black Death. Its sister plague was actually more virulent. Although some people survived after having the Black Death, the second type of plague had 100% mortality rate. Some theorists believe that anthrax was the cause. Both plagues decimated the population and broke down the feudal system. There were no longer enough people to work the land, and no longer enough landlords to ensure that vassals were 'kept in their place'. The whole of England was plunged into chaos, and by the time the population had found its feet again, feudalism, the system under which a landowner also 'owned' his tenants, was beginning to break down.

All Saints Church retains evidence of early Saxon architecture. The building as we see it today is believed to have been completed in three main stages. The primary Anglo-Saxon structure used red sandstone and was considerably smaller. Later Norman and then 14th century re-constructions used limestone to expand the church. Some local historians believe that the Saxon building could have been destroyed when Earl Edwin was implicated in an early Saxon rebellion. After the Conquest, the ruling Normans did not take kindly to uprisings, and acted brutally to suppress freedom-fighters and rebels. If this was the case, then much of old Laughton could have been destroyed in the ensuing battle. All Saints lay in ruins for fifty years at one point before being restored to the structure we see today.

Its choice of name is also telling; Saxon churches are often named 'all saints' or 'all hallows' rather than being named after a particular saint, as was later the case. This could be due to the lack of genuine 'relics' available at this point in history. Shortly afterwards, all manner of faked 'bones of the saints' and fragments of their clothes were put in cabinets on many altars, and subsequent churches were either created in their honour or named after them.

There was an old custom among the locals of Laughton that the top of the spire was a 'sea-mark'. This probably meant that they thought people as far as the coast could see the top of it. All Saints is certainly visible for miles around, being on the top of a large hill. One historian has remarked that Laughton-en-le-Morthing (to give it its old title) was often mistakenly written on maps as 'Lighten-in-the-morning' because the sight of the church struck by sunlight was so memorable.

Early one morning in the mid-1980's, Mr Anthony Lee was riding his moped past the Gallows public house on his way to work in Thurcroft. He had come through Dinnington in a slight mist, although this was not so thick as to make visibility too difficult. He drew up behind an old-fashioned closed carriage being pulled by horses.

He was close enough to the back of the carriage to see it clearly, and although Mr Lee thought that it was unusual to see an outdated vehicle such as this, he was aware that they were still being used for publicity purposes and sometimes even for pleasure by local people from the surrounding villages. However, his interest turned to amazement as they drew close to the railway bridge. Instead of following the contour of the road and going over the raised bridge, the carriage carried on at the same level and drove straight through it, disappearing bit by bit!

Many years ago, before the bridge was constructed over the railway, the road had indeed been on one level. At the time of the railway construction, the road had been raised at this point to accommodate trains which were to carry coal underneath. The ghostly carriage was evidently continuing along its original route!

The Gallows public house marks the spot where wrongdoers were executed in Laughton as an example to the rest of society. Traditionally, gallows were situated on a crossroads so that the spirit of the sinner could not find its way to the next world. Crossroads are also associated with the Devil for this reason. The Gallows pub is situated next to an old crossroads. Hangsman Lane passes the pub, and even one of the more modern shops is named after 'Hangsman'! Not surprisingly, the gallows was such a focus of local fear that the folk memory finds it hard to forget places such as this, even when they have gone out of use. However, the current Gallows landlord says he is not aware of any strange happenings in or around the building, despite the history of the place!

LAST WORDS

It has always been easy for sceptics to scoff at supernatural matters, or laugh at unexplained events recounted by others. But just remember that, as soon as the sun goes down, a door into another more frightening world can be opened... and a strange light in the darkness, a mysterious cry, or the hooting of an owl can suddenly take on an altogether more sinister association.

How many disbelievers out there would volunteer to be alone in a derelict Abbey as the clock strikes midnight? Reply truthfully, and there you have your answer...

Liz Linahan, 1994

Bibliography

The following books proved interesting and useful in researching Pit Ghosts, Padfeet and Poltergeists:

Magilton, J.R. *Doncaster District: an archaeological Survey* Doncaster Museums and Arts Service

Hunter, J. *South Yorkshire* Vols I & II J B Nicholls & Son

Robinson-Walsh, D. (Ed.) *Stories and Tales of Old Yorkshire* Printwise publications

Drinkwater, J: *Changing Village* Rotherham Libraries

Cunniff, T. *The Supernatural in Yorkshire* Dalesman

Fletcher, J.S. *Memories of a Spectator*

Machin, F. *The Yorkshire Miners, A History* N.U.M.

Maple, E. *The Realm of Ghosts*

Tomlin, A.R. *Local Folk Lore* The Barnsley Chronicle, 1894

Vernon, F. *Pride and Poverty, Memories of a Mexborough Miner*

Workers Educational Association *History in Laughton-en-Le-Morthen* Rotherham Libraries

Workers Educational Association *Anston (North and South)* Rotherham Libraries

Young, R: *The Parish of Dinnington* Sissons & Son Ltd

I would also like to thank the following people for their help:

Brian Elliott, who kindly contributed a foreword, Barnsley Library & Archives, Dinnington Local History Library, Karen Baker for drawing some of the illustrations, Nick Briggs and Raychel Perks for layout, design and cover work, Maisie Robson for proof reading the manuscript, and Phillip Rendell, whose idea it was.

In addition, I would like to thank *all* the people, too numerous to mention individually here, who contributed the stories which made this book possible.